Electronics for Beginners

Building Circuits and Learning Hardware Basics Learn the fundamentals of circuits, resistors, and microcontrollers

THOMPSON CARTER

All rights reserved

Table of Content

TABLE OF CONTENTS

Introduction

Electronics for Beginners: Building Circuits and Learning Hardware Basics

Welcome to *"Electronics for Beginners: Building Circuits and Learning Hardware Basics"*. Whether you're looking to understand the fundamental principles of electronics or aiming to develop the hands-on skills to bring your own ideas to life, this book will be your guide on that exciting journey. Electronics is a vast and ever-evolving field, and this book is designed to equip you with the foundational knowledge and practical experience you need to succeed in your electronic endeavors.

In the modern world, electronics has become an integral part of nearly everything we interact with. From the smallest wearables like smartwatches to the most complex systems such as artificial intelligence applications, electronics is the backbone of all technological advancements. Understanding how circuits work, how to manipulate electronic components, and how to integrate them into functional systems opens the door to a world of creativity and problem-solving.

This book is meant to be a comprehensive, step-by-step resource for anyone starting their journey in electronics, with no prior experience necessary. The approach is structured and beginner-friendly, providing clear explanations and real-world examples to help you grasp the core concepts and master essential techniques. Along the way, you'll learn the key components of electronic circuits—resistors, capacitors, diodes, transistors, and more—and understand how these components work together to create functional devices.

Why This Book?

One of the most exciting things about electronics is how easily you can experiment with different components to create new and innovative projects. This book encourages active learning through hands-on activities and real-world examples. It not only explains the theory behind electronics but also guides you through practical projects to help you apply what you've learned. The book includes a wide range of projects, starting from simple circuits and gradually progressing to more advanced systems like microcontroller-based projects, IoT devices, and wireless communication setups.

You'll start by learning the essential components of a circuit, how to use them, and how to read circuit diagrams. From there, we'll dive deeper into more complex topics, such as working with sensors and actuators, understanding the role of microcontrollers, and controlling devices through wireless communication technologies like Bluetooth and Wi-Fi.

By the time you finish this book, you'll not only have a solid understanding of the key principles of electronics, but you'll also have gained the confidence to design and build your own projects, troubleshoot circuits, and optimize your designs for performance. The ultimate goal is to inspire creativity and problem-solving skills in every reader, so you can take the concepts you learn here and apply them to your own projects, whatever they may be.

Who is This Book For?

This book is for anyone with an interest in electronics, whether you're a student, hobbyist, or professional looking to refresh your knowledge. You don't need a background in electrical engineering to benefit from this book—just a curiosity to learn and a passion for experimenting with technology. Whether you're interested in creating DIY projects, building embedded systems, developing IoT devices, or just understanding how everyday gadgets work, this book will guide you through each step of the learning process.

If you're a complete beginner with no prior knowledge of electronics, don't worry. We'll start with the basics, such as understanding voltage, current, and resistance, and build from there. Each chapter is designed to help you master one core concept before moving on to the next, ensuring you feel confident in your understanding of each topic.

What Will You Learn?

Here's a brief outline of the key skills and concepts you'll learn in this book:

1. **Basic Components and Their Functions**: You will learn about the essential building blocks of electronic circuits, such as resistors, capacitors, diodes, transistors, and more. You'll understand how they work individually and how they work together to form complex systems.

2. **Circuit Design and Prototyping**: You'll gain hands-on experience building simple circuits, using

breadboards, and learning how to read and create circuit diagrams.

3. **Microcontrollers and Programming**: A major focus of this book is understanding how microcontrollers (like Arduino and Raspberry Pi) interact with electronic components. You'll learn how to program microcontrollers to control sensors, actuators, and devices.

4. **Working with Sensors and Actuators**: You'll explore how sensors gather information from the environment (e.g., temperature, motion, light) and how actuators respond to control signals (e.g., motors, servos, relays).

5. **Wireless Communication**: As electronics become more interconnected, wireless communication plays an essential role. You'll learn how to use Bluetooth, Wi-Fi, and RF communication to control devices remotely and build IoT (Internet of Things) systems.

6. **Troubleshooting and Repairing Circuits**: We'll dive into the essential skill of troubleshooting— learning how to diagnose and repair common circuit problems, ensuring your projects work as intended.

7. **Building and Sharing Your Projects**: Finally, you'll discover how to document, share, and

collaborate on your projects with others. Open-source communities and online platforms provide an excellent opportunity for makers to share their work, get feedback, and improve.

Why Now?

The world is more connected than ever before. With the rise of smart homes, wearable tech, and IoT devices, electronics has become a critical part of daily life. As the world continues to become more automated and interconnected, the demand for individuals who understand electronics is only going to grow. This book equips you with the skills necessary to be a part of that exciting future.

Whether you want to build a home automation system, create a wearable gadget, or dive into the world of robotics and IoT, this book will provide you with the tools and knowledge to take on any electronics project you can imagine. The future is full of exciting possibilities, and with the right foundation, you can be part of shaping that future.

Conclusion

By the end of this book, you will have a thorough understanding of how electronic circuits work and how to build your own projects. From the most basic concepts to advanced applications in wireless communication and IoT, this book covers it all. So, get ready to experiment, learn, and create—your journey into the world of electronics begins now.

CHAPTER 1

INTRODUCTION TO ELECTRONICS

What is Electronics?

Electronics is the branch of science and technology that deals with the design and application of circuits, devices, and systems that use electrical energy to perform various functions. At its core, electronics is about controlling the flow of electric current to create, store, and transfer information, or perform tasks like heating, lighting, or sound production. Essentially, it focuses on how to manipulate electrical signals to achieve specific purposes.

In electronics, we use components such as resistors, capacitors, diodes, transistors, and microcontrollers to build systems that can process signals and control power. Unlike electrical engineering, which deals with the generation and transmission of electrical energy, electronics is more focused on how that energy is used in devices to perform tasks.

Basic Components of Electronic Circuits

To understand electronics, it's important to familiarize yourself with the fundamental components used in building electronic circuits. Each component has a unique role, and together they make up the foundation of all electronic systems.

- **Resistors**: Resistors limit or control the flow of electrical current in a circuit. They are essential for ensuring that components receive the appropriate amount of power. For example, a resistor is used to protect LEDs by limiting the current that flows through them.

- **Capacitors**: Capacitors store electrical energy temporarily and release it when needed. They are used for smoothing voltage fluctuations, filtering signals, and timing applications. In power supplies, capacitors help stabilize the voltage output.

- **Diodes**: Diodes are components that allow current to flow in only one direction, providing a path for current in one direction while blocking it in the other. They are often used in rectifiers, which convert AC (alternating current) to DC (direct current).

- **Transistors**: Transistors act as switches or amplifiers. They can turn on or off the flow of current or amplify signals. Transistors are the building blocks of modern electronics and are used in everything from computers to smartphones.

- **Microcontrollers**: Microcontrollers are small computers on a single chip. They can be programmed to perform a variety of tasks, such as controlling motors, reading sensor data, or managing communication between different devices.

These components are often combined to create circuits that perform specific tasks, like turning on a light or processing data.

Real-World Examples of Electronics in Daily Life

Electronics are an integral part of our daily lives, and we interact with them in countless ways without always realizing it. Here are some everyday examples of how electronics impact us:

- **Smartphones**: Smartphones are packed with electronic circuits and components like microcontrollers, sensors, and transistors. They allow us to communicate, access the internet, and use countless apps, all thanks to complex electronics working together seamlessly.

- **Home Appliances**: From refrigerators and washing machines to microwaves and air conditioners, electronics control many of the functions in our home appliances. Microcontrollers manage the temperature in your fridge, sensors detect when clothes are clean in your washing machine, and digital timers control the cooking time in a microwave.

- **Cars**: Modern cars rely heavily on electronics. From engine management systems and airbags to GPS navigation and entertainment systems, electronics ensure that everything functions smoothly and efficiently in your vehicle.

- **Wearable Devices**: Fitness trackers, smartwatches, and health monitors all rely on electronic components to track activity, heart rate, and other health metrics. These devices use sensors, microcontrollers, and communication circuits to process data and sync with your smartphone.

- **Entertainment Systems**: Your TV, speakers, gaming consoles, and streaming devices all use electronics to display images, process audio, and communicate with networks. Transistors, capacitors, and microcontrollers are essential in making your entertainment devices function.

From the light switches in your home to the smartphones in your pocket, electronics make life easier, more efficient, and often more enjoyable. Understanding the basics of how these devices work opens the door to creating your own electronic projects, whether for personal use or as part of a career in electronics.

This chapter provides a solid foundation for understanding what electronics are and introduces the fundamental components that will be used throughout the book.

CHAPTER 2

UNDERSTANDING VOLTAGE, CURRENT, AND RESISTANCE

The Relationship Between Voltage, Current, and Resistance

To build and understand electronic circuits, it's crucial to grasp the fundamental relationship between three key electrical properties: **voltage**, **current**, and **resistance**. These three factors work together to control the behavior of electrical circuits.

- **Voltage (V)**: Voltage is the electrical potential difference between two points in a circuit. It is what pushes the current through the circuit, much like water pressure pushing water through a pipe. Voltage is measured in **volts (V)**.
- **Current (I)**: Current is the flow of electric charge through a conductor (like a wire). It is measured in **amperes (A)**. When a voltage is applied to a circuit, it causes current to flow. You can think of current as the rate at which electrons move through a circuit.

- **Resistance (R)**: Resistance is the opposition to the flow of current in a circuit. It's like friction in a pipe that resists the flow of water. Resistance is measured in **ohms (Ω)**. Materials with high resistance, like rubber, prevent the flow of electricity, while materials with low resistance, like copper, allow it to flow easily.

The relationship between voltage, current, and resistance is best understood using **Ohm's Law**, which provides a simple formula to calculate the value of one of these properties if the other two are known:

$V = I \times R$

This means:

- Voltage (V) equals current (I) multiplied by resistance (R).
- If you know two of these values, you can easily calculate the third.

Ohm's Law and Its Importance in Circuit Design

Ohm's Law is fundamental in electronics because it allows you to design circuits that function predictably. It helps you understand how different components in a circuit affect each other and how to control the flow of current.

For example, if you have a circuit with a known voltage and resistance, you can use Ohm's Law to calculate the current that will flow through the circuit. Conversely, if you know the current and resistance, you can calculate the voltage.

In practical terms, Ohm's Law helps in:

- **Choosing the right resistors**: If you need to limit current in a circuit, Ohm's Law allows you to choose the correct resistor size. For instance, if you want to limit the current through an LED to 20 mA, Ohm's Law will tell you the appropriate resistor to use given the voltage of your power supply.
- **Understanding power consumption**: Ohm's Law also ties into power, as power (P) is equal to voltage (V) multiplied by current (I). This allows you to calculate how much energy a circuit consumes, which is vital for designing energy-efficient systems.
- **Troubleshooting circuits**: If a circuit isn't working as expected, you can use Ohm's Law to check if the voltage and current values are correct and diagnose

potential issues like too much resistance or insufficient voltage.

Ohm's Law is one of the first tools you'll use when designing and analyzing circuits, and understanding it thoroughly is crucial for building reliable and efficient electronics.

Real-World Example: How a Lightbulb Works

Let's use the example of a **lightbulb** to demonstrate how voltage, current, and resistance interact in a circuit.

When you turn on a light, electricity flows through the filament inside the bulb. Here's how each of the three properties plays a role:

- **Voltage**: The voltage from the power source (usually 120V or 220V depending on your country's electrical system) is applied to the lightbulb.
- **Current**: The voltage causes the current to flow through the filament of the lightbulb. The filament, usually made of tungsten, resists the flow of electricity. This resistance causes the filament to heat up.
- **Resistance**: The tungsten filament has a specific resistance that controls how much current can flow

through it. The higher the resistance, the less current flows for a given voltage. The filament's resistance causes it to heat up to a point where it starts glowing, producing light.

Using Ohm's Law, we can calculate the current flowing through the bulb. For instance, if the bulb has a resistance of 240 ohms and the supply voltage is 120V, the current flowing through the bulb would be:

I=VR=120240=0.5 AI = \frac{V}{R} = \frac{120}{240} = 0.5 \, \text{A}I=RV=240120=0.5A

This shows that the current flowing through the lightbulb is 0.5 amperes when it is connected to a 120V power source. The filament's resistance controls how much current flows, and the heat generated by the resistance makes the bulb light up.

This basic principle of voltage, current, and resistance is not just confined to lightbulbs but applies to every electronic device that uses electricity. Understanding how these three properties work together will help you design circuits and troubleshoot electronic systems effectively.

This chapter introduces you to the core concepts of electricity, setting the stage for more complex circuit designs. By understanding the relationships between voltage, current, and resistance, you'll be ready to tackle basic circuits and start building your own electronic projects.

CHAPTER 3

EXPLORING RESISTORS

What Are Resistors and Their Purpose in Circuits?

A **resistor** is a basic electrical component used in electronic circuits to limit or control the flow of electric current. In simple terms, resistors "resist" the flow of current, and they are essential for managing the amount of electricity that flows through various parts of a circuit.

The purpose of resistors in circuits includes:

- **Limiting Current**: Resistors are often used to reduce or limit the current that flows through sensitive components like LEDs (Light Emitting Diodes). Without a resistor, the current could be too high, potentially damaging the LED.
- **Voltage Division**: In circuits with multiple components, resistors can divide voltage in a predictable manner. By placing resistors in series or parallel, you can control how much voltage is dropped across each component.

- **Signal Processing**: In analog circuits, resistors can help in filtering signals, such as controlling the response of audio equipment or managing sensor signals.

Resistors are often used in almost every type of electronic device, from simple home electronics to complex microprocessor systems, making them fundamental components in circuit design.

Types of Resistors

There are several different types of resistors, each designed for specific applications. Some of the most common types include:

- **Fixed Resistors**: These resistors have a set resistance value that cannot be changed. They are the most common type and come in various forms, such as carbon-film resistors, metal oxide resistors, and wire-wound resistors.
  - o **Carbon Film Resistors**: These are cheap and commonly used in everyday electronics. They are made by placing a thin layer of carbon on an insulating material, with the resistance value

determined by the thickness and length of the carbon layer.

- o **Metal Oxide Resistors**: These resistors are more stable and reliable than carbon film resistors. They are used in circuits where stability and accuracy are essential.

- o **Wire-Wound Resistors**: These are typically used in high-power applications and consist of a wire (usually made of metal) wound around an insulating core. They are capable of handling high currents and dissipating heat.

- **Variable Resistors (Potentiometers and Rheostats)**: Unlike fixed resistors, variable resistors allow you to adjust the resistance value manually. They are used in applications where you need to control the flow of current or voltage dynamically.

  - o **Potentiometer**: A three-terminal resistor with a rotating knob or slider that adjusts the resistance between two terminals. It is commonly used for volume control in audio equipment or as a user interface for adjusting settings in electronic devices.

  - o **Rheostat**: A two-terminal variable resistor used to control current in a circuit, typically used for adjusting the brightness of lights or the speed of motors.

- **Surface-Mount Resistors**: These are small resistors designed for mounting directly onto the surface of a circuit board, rather than through holes. They are common in modern electronic devices because they take up less space and are more suitable for automated manufacturing processes.

- **Specialty Resistors**: In certain applications, resistors with specific properties, such as high precision or high power rating, are required. These resistors are often used in industrial or scientific equipment.

How to Choose the Right Resistor for Your Circuit

Choosing the right resistor for your circuit is crucial for ensuring that your circuit operates correctly and efficiently. Here's how to select the appropriate resistor for a project:

1. **Determine the Required Resistance Value**: The first step in choosing a resistor is determining the resistance needed for the circuit. This depends on the specifications of the components you're working with and the desired current flow. For example, if you are connecting an LED to a power supply, you need to calculate the resistor value that will limit the current to a safe level.

You can calculate the resistance needed using **Ohm's Law**:

R=VIR = \frac{V}{I}R=IV

Where:

- o **R** is the resistance in ohms (Ω)
- o **V** is the voltage across the resistor
- o **I** is the desired current

For example, if you have a 9V battery and an LED that requires 20mA of current, the resistor needed would be:

R=9V0.02A=450 ΩR = \frac{9V}{0.02A} = 450 \, \OmegaR=0.02A9V=450Ω

So, you would choose a resistor with a resistance of 450 ohms.

2. **Consider Power Rating**: Every resistor has a maximum power rating, which indicates how much power it can safely dissipate without getting damaged. The power dissipated by a resistor is calculated using:

$$P=I2\times RP = I^\wedge 2 \text{ \textbackslash times } RP=I2\times R$$

Where **P** is the power in watts (W), **I** is the current through the resistor, and **R** is the resistance.

For example, if your circuit uses 20mA (0.02A) of current and a 450-ohm resistor, the power dissipated would be:

$$P=(0.02A)2\times450 \ \Omega=0.18 \ WP = (0.02A)^\wedge 2 \text{ \textbackslash times } 450 \text{ \textbackslash},$$
$$\text{\textbackslash Omega} = 0.18 \text{ \textbackslash}, \ WP=(0.02A)2\times450\Omega=0.18W$$

In this case, you would choose a resistor with a power rating of at least 0.25W (to provide a margin of safety).

3. **Choose the Right Tolerance**: Tolerance refers to how much a resistor's actual resistance can vary from its labeled value. For most everyday circuits, a tolerance of 5% is sufficient. However, for precision applications, you may need resistors with a tighter tolerance, such as 1% or even 0.1%.

4. **Check for Temperature Coefficient**: The temperature coefficient of a resistor indicates how much its resistance changes with temperature. This is especially important in environments where

temperature fluctuates significantly. If your circuit will operate in such conditions, make sure to select resistors with a low temperature coefficient.

5. **Physical Size and Type**: Depending on your project, you may need to choose between through-hole resistors (for breadboards and prototyping) or surface-mount resistors (for compact, high-density designs). Consider the space available on your circuit board and the ease of handling when selecting the resistor type.

By carefully considering these factors, you can select the right resistor that ensures your circuit works as expected, is energy-efficient, and operates within safe limits.

In this chapter, you've learned the essential role of resistors in controlling current flow and how to choose the right type of resistor for your projects. Whether you're building a simple LED circuit or working on a more complex design, resistors are an essential component to understand and use effectively.

CHAPTER 4

CAPACITORS AND THEIR ROLE IN CIRCUITS

What Are Capacitors?

A **capacitor** is an electronic component that stores electrical energy temporarily and releases it when needed. It consists of two conductive plates separated by an insulating material known as the **dielectric**. When a voltage is applied across the plates, the capacitor accumulates electrical charge on its plates. The amount of charge a capacitor can store depends on its **capacitance**, which is measured in **farads (F)**.

Capacitors are commonly used in electronic circuits to smooth out voltage fluctuations, filter signals, store energy, and control timing in circuits. Unlike resistors, which resist the flow of current, capacitors allow current to flow in certain ways, making them crucial for various applications, from power management to signal processing.

The core function of a capacitor is to **charge** and **discharge**: it stores energy when there is an excess and releases it when required, helping to maintain a consistent power supply or smooth signal.

Types of Capacitors and Their Uses

There are several types of capacitors, each suited for different applications based on their construction and material properties. Some of the most common types include:

- **Ceramic Capacitors**: These are among the most widely used capacitors and are made from a ceramic material as the dielectric. They are small, inexpensive, and come in a variety of capacitance values. Ceramic capacitors are commonly used in high-frequency circuits like radio receivers, as well as for filtering and decoupling power supplies.

- **Electrolytic Capacitors**: Electrolytic capacitors have a very high capacitance value relative to their size, making them ideal for power applications where large amounts of energy storage are required. These capacitors use an electrolyte as one of the plates and are polarized, meaning they must be installed in the correct orientation. They are commonly used in power supply filters, decoupling, and smoothing applications.

- **Tantalum Capacitors**: Tantalum capacitors are similar to electrolytic capacitors but are more stable and reliable. They are made from a tantalum metal anode and have a higher capacitance per volume than ceramic capacitors. Tantalum capacitors are often used in power supply circuits and applications requiring higher capacitance and small size.

- **Film Capacitors**: Film capacitors use a thin plastic film as the dielectric and are known for their stability, reliability, and low loss. They come in different varieties such as polyester, polypropylene, and polycarbonate, and are often used in precision applications like audio equipment, timing circuits, and filters.

- **Supercapacitors (Ultracapacitors)**: Supercapacitors are specialized capacitors with very high capacitance values, sometimes measured in farads or even thousands of farads. They are used for applications that require rapid charge and discharge cycles, such as in memory backup systems, regenerative braking in electric vehicles, and power smoothing in renewable energy systems.

Each of these capacitors has specific characteristics that make them suitable for different tasks. For example, electrolytic capacitors are ideal for applications where high capacitance is needed in a small size, while ceramic capacitors are great for high-frequency circuits.

Real-World Example: Capacitors in Power Supplies

One of the most common uses of capacitors is in **power supply circuits**, where they play a critical role in ensuring that the voltage remains stable and smooth. Power supplies, particularly those converting AC (alternating current) to DC (direct current), often experience fluctuations in voltage, which can lead to instability or failure in the powered devices.

In a **rectifier circuit**, which converts AC to DC, capacitors are used to smooth the rectified output. When AC is converted to DC, the output voltage is not constant; it contains ripples or fluctuations. This ripple can be problematic for sensitive electronics, which require a steady DC voltage to operate correctly.

Here's how capacitors help in this process:

1. **Filtering**: After the AC is converted into pulsating DC by the rectifier, a capacitor is placed across the output. The capacitor charges during the peaks of the AC signal and discharges during the valleys. This charging and discharging action smooth out the fluctuations, reducing the ripple and providing a more stable DC output.

2. **Energy Storage**: Capacitors also act as short-term energy reservoirs. When there is a sudden demand for power, such as when a device suddenly draws more current, capacitors can supply the required charge quickly, helping to maintain a stable voltage in the circuit.

3. **Voltage Regulation**: Capacitors are used in conjunction with other components like voltage regulators to maintain a consistent voltage output. In high-quality power supplies, several stages of capacitors (using different capacitances) are used to filter, smooth, and regulate the voltage to the desired level.

For example, in a **computer power supply**, the input AC is converted into DC through a rectifier. Capacitors are then used to smooth the DC voltage and remove any residual ripple. These capacitors allow the computer to receive a clean, stable DC voltage, ensuring that the sensitive components inside the computer, like the motherboard and processor, receive consistent power and operate properly.

Conclusion

Capacitors are fundamental components in electronics, used to store energy, filter signals, and smooth out voltage fluctuations. They come in various types, each designed for specific applications, ranging from small ceramic capacitors to high-capacity supercapacitors. Understanding how capacitors function and how to select the right one for your circuit is crucial in building reliable and efficient electronic systems.

By using capacitors effectively, you can enhance the performance of power supplies, improve signal integrity, and ensure that your circuits operate without interruptions. Whether you're building a simple project or designing complex electronics, capacitors are indispensable tools in your toolkit.

CHAPTER 5

UNDERSTANDING DIODES AND TRANSISTORS

What Are Diodes and Transistors?

Diodes and **transistors** are two of the most important components in electronic circuits. Both devices are essential for controlling the flow of current and shaping the behavior of circuits. Here's a closer look at each:

- **Diodes**: A diode is a semiconductor device that allows current to flow in only one direction while blocking it in the opposite direction. This is why diodes are often referred to as **unidirectional** devices. A diode typically has two terminals: the **anode** (positive side) and the **cathode** (negative side). Current can only flow from the anode to the cathode, and if the current tries to flow in the reverse direction, the diode will block it. This makes diodes essential for applications where controlling the direction of current flow is necessary.

○ **Types of Diodes**: The most common types of diodes include:

- **Standard diodes**: Used for basic rectification in power supplies.

- **Zener diodes**: Special diodes that allow current to flow in the reverse direction when a specific voltage (called the "Zener voltage") is reached, often used in voltage regulation circuits.

- **Light Emitting Diodes (LEDs)**: A type of diode that emits light when current flows through it. LEDs are widely used in displays, indicators, and lighting applications.

- **Transistors**: A transistor is a semiconductor device that can amplify signals or act as a switch to control the flow of current. A transistor has three terminals: **emitter**, **base**, and **collector**. By applying a small current to the base terminal, a transistor allows a larger current to flow between the emitter and collector. This ability to control large currents with small input signals makes transistors essential in amplifying signals in electronic devices such as radios, TVs, and computers.

o **Types of Transistors**: The most commonly used types of transistors are:

- **Bipolar Junction Transistors (BJTs)**: BJTs are used to amplify current. They come in two types: NPN and PNP transistors. The main difference is the arrangement of the semiconductor material.

- **Field-Effect Transistors (FETs)**: FETs control current flow by using an electric field. They are used in a wide range of applications, including amplifiers, signal processing, and digital circuits.

Their Role in Controlling the Flow of Current

- **Diodes in Current Control**: Diodes play a crucial role in controlling the direction of current flow. In simple terms, they act as **one-way gates** for electric current. For instance, in a **rectifier circuit**, which converts AC (alternating current) into DC (direct current), diodes allow current to flow only during the positive half-cycle of the AC signal, blocking current flow during the negative half-cycle. This process results in **pulsating DC**, which can be further smoothed using capacitors.

40

Diodes also help prevent damage to sensitive components by blocking unwanted reverse current, ensuring that the current only flows where it is needed. They are essential for protecting circuits from overvoltage or incorrect power direction.

- **Transistors in Current Control**: Transistors are used for both **amplification** and **switching**. In amplification, a small current at the base terminal controls a much larger current flowing between the emitter and collector. This property makes transistors vital in devices like radios, microphones, and audio equipment, where weak signals need to be amplified to a level suitable for output.

In switching applications, transistors act as electronic switches, allowing or blocking the flow of current between two terminals. For example, a transistor can switch on a light, control the timing of a signal, or even be used in logic circuits as the fundamental building block of digital computers.

Practical Applications: Rectifiers and Amplifiers

- **Rectifiers**: Rectifiers are circuits that convert AC to DC. Diodes are the key components in rectifiers. In a simple **half-wave rectifier**, a single diode is used to allow current to flow only during the positive half-cycle of an AC signal, effectively blocking the negative half-cycle. The result is a pulsating DC signal.

  In a **full-wave rectifier**, two diodes are used, allowing both the positive and negative halves of the AC signal to be converted into a usable DC signal. More advanced rectifier circuits use **bridge rectifiers**, which incorporate four diodes arranged in a bridge configuration for higher efficiency and smoother DC output.

  Real-World Example: In power supplies for electronic devices, rectifiers are used to convert the AC from the electrical outlet into the DC needed by the device. Without diodes in the rectifier, the electronics would not receive the correct form of power and would fail to operate.

- **Amplifiers**: Transistors are widely used in **amplifiers** to increase the amplitude of weak electrical signals. The transistor amplifies a small input signal, which is then used to drive speakers, display screens, or other output devices.

- o **Common-Emitter Amplifier**: A basic type of amplifier circuit using a BJT transistor, where the input signal is applied to the base, and the output is taken from the collector. This configuration is popular in audio amplification systems, such as in **guitar amplifiers** or **home audio systems**.

- o **Operational Amplifiers (Op-Amps)**: Op-amps are specialized transistors that are designed to amplify signals in a variety of applications, including audio processing, signal filtering, and feedback loops in control systems. They are used in everything from hearing aids to radar systems.

Real-World Example: In a **microphone amplifier**, a small sound signal is picked up by the microphone, and the transistor amplifies this signal to a level strong enough to drive speakers or be processed by other audio equipment. Without transistors in the amplifier, the sound signal would be too weak to be heard by the human ear.

Transistors and diodes are foundational to the electronics that power modern technology. Their ability to control the flow of current makes them indispensable in everything from power supplies to communication systems.

This chapter introduces you to the world of diodes and transistors, showing their critical role in current control, rectification, and amplification. Understanding how these components work in practical applications helps you build and troubleshoot electronic circuits with confidence.

CHAPTER 6

INTRODUCTION TO CIRCUIT DESIGN

Basic Principles of Designing Circuits

Designing electronic circuits involves understanding how components interact with each other to perform a specific function. Whether you are designing a simple light circuit or a complex audio amplifier, following a few key principles can help ensure your design is effective, reliable, and easy to troubleshoot.

Here are some basic principles of circuit design:

1. **Understand the Purpose**: Before beginning, clearly define what the circuit is supposed to do. Are you designing a power supply, a signal amplifier, or a simple on/off switch? Knowing the end goal will help you choose the right components and design the layout accordingly.

2. **Component Selection**: Choose the right components based on the requirements of the circuit. For

example, resistors should be selected to limit current to safe levels, capacitors for filtering or energy storage, and transistors for amplification or switching. Always ensure that components can handle the voltage and current your circuit will supply.

3. **Current and Voltage Flow**: Always be mindful of how current and voltage flow in a circuit. You need to ensure that components receive the correct voltage and current to operate efficiently. For example, placing a resistor in series with an LED limits the current to prevent burning it out, and using capacitors to smooth out voltage fluctuations keeps your circuit stable.

4. **Power Considerations**: Pay attention to how much power your components will dissipate. Some components, like resistors, can get quite hot if too much current passes through them. Choose components that match the power requirements of your circuit and ensure they won't overheat or cause damage.

5. **Signal Integrity**: In more advanced designs, maintaining clean signals is crucial. For example, in audio circuits, filtering out unwanted noise or

interference is essential to ensure high-quality sound output. This might involve using capacitors, inductors, or shielding to preserve signal integrity.

6. **Prototyping First**: It's always a good idea to build a prototype of your circuit before finalizing the design. This allows you to test the functionality and identify any issues early in the process, saving you time and money in the long run.

Using Breadboards for Prototyping

A **breadboard** is a handy tool for prototyping and testing circuits without soldering components to a printed circuit board (PCB). It allows you to quickly and easily assemble and modify your circuit, making it ideal for experimentation and learning.

- **What is a Breadboard?**: A breadboard is a rectangular, plastic board with a grid of holes that are connected in rows and columns. The rows and columns are electrically connected, which allows components to be inserted into the holes and form a complete circuit.

- **How to Use a Breadboard**:

- o Components like resistors, capacitors, diodes, and integrated circuits (ICs) can be inserted into the breadboard. Each row of holes is connected together, making it easy to connect components without needing to solder.
- o For example, when placing an LED on the breadboard, you would insert the anode (longer leg) into one row and the cathode (shorter leg) into a different row. A resistor can then be connected between the anode and the power supply to limit the current.
- o Breadboards also have **power rails** (usually marked with a red and blue line) where you can easily insert the positive (red) and ground (blue) connections from your power supply.

- **Why Use a Breadboard?**:
  - o Breadboards are a flexible and fast way to build and test circuits. You can easily modify your circuit by moving components around or swapping parts out, making them perfect for rapid prototyping.
  - o They are reusable, which means you can use the same breadboard for multiple projects. This helps you save money on printed circuit boards while still being able to test and refine your designs.

Breadboards are particularly useful when you're just starting out with circuit design, as they make it easy to experiment with different component values and configurations before committing to a final design.

How to Draw and Understand Circuit Diagrams

Circuit diagrams are a graphical representation of an electronic circuit. They show how components are connected and how electrical current flows between them. Understanding how to read and create these diagrams is crucial for designing and troubleshooting circuits.

1. **Basic Symbols**: Each component in a circuit has its own unique symbol. Some common symbols include:
    o **Resistor**: A zigzag line or rectangle.
    o **Capacitor**: Two parallel lines with a gap between them (for non-polarized capacitors), or one line and one curved line (for polarized capacitors).
    o **Diode**: A triangle pointing to a line (representing the direction of current flow).
    o **Transistor**: A combination of lines and arrows representing the emitter, base, and collector terminals.

- o **Power Source**: A pair of lines, with the longer line representing the positive terminal and the shorter line representing the negative terminal.

2. **Reading Circuit Diagrams**:
   - o **Connections**: Circuit diagrams show how the components are electrically connected. Lines represent wires or traces that carry the current.
   - o **Flow of Current**: Arrows may be used to show the direction of current flow, although the actual direction of current in a circuit is usually from positive to negative (conventional current flow).
   - o **Ground and Power**: Power sources and ground connections are typically shown at the top and bottom of the diagram. Ground is often represented by a set of horizontal lines stacked on top of each other.

3. **Creating Circuit Diagrams**:
   - o Start by drawing the power supply and ground, then add the components that will be part of your circuit.
   - o Use straight lines for the connections between components, ensuring that they don't overlap or cross unless they are meant to.
   - o Label all components clearly, especially resistors, capacitors, and transistors, to help you understand the values and functionality at a glance.

4. **Simplifying Circuit Design**:

- o While designing a circuit, it's important to keep the diagram simple and organized. Group related components together, use labels for important components, and avoid cluttering the diagram with unnecessary details.
- o Use software tools like **Fritzing**, **Tinkercad**, or **KiCad** to create clean, professional-looking circuit diagrams, especially for more complex projects.

Understanding circuit diagrams is an essential skill for anyone working with electronics. By visualizing your design in diagram form, you can more easily see how the components will interact and make adjustments as needed before physically assembling the circuit.

In this chapter, you've learned the basics of circuit design, including how to prototype on a breadboard and create circuit diagrams. These skills will lay the foundation for building more complex circuits as you progress in your electronics journey. By following the principles of good design and using tools like breadboards and circuit diagrams, you'll be well on your way to creating effective and reliable electronic systems.

CHAPTER 7

SOLDERING BASICS AND TOOLS

Introduction to Soldering

Soldering is the process of joining two or more metal components together using a filler metal called **solder**. The solder melts at a lower temperature than the components being joined, allowing the metal parts to be securely bonded without damaging them. Soldering is a fundamental skill in electronics, and it's used to connect components on a **printed circuit board (PCB)**, create wire connections, and build more permanent electronic circuits.

The two main types of soldering are:

- **Through-hole Soldering**: This is the traditional method where components have leads (pins) that pass through holes in a PCB. The leads are soldered on the other side of the board.
- **Surface-mount Soldering**: In modern electronics, many components are designed to be soldered onto the surface of the PCB rather than through holes. This method is commonly used in mass production.

Soldering is an essential skill for building and repairing circuits, and mastering it will enable you to work on everything from DIY electronics projects to more advanced circuit design.

Essential Tools for Soldering

Before you begin soldering, it's important to have the right tools to ensure clean, safe, and efficient soldering. Here are the essential tools you'll need:

1. **Soldering Iron**:
    o The soldering iron is the primary tool used to heat and melt the solder. It consists of a handle with a heated metal tip. You'll need to choose a soldering iron with an appropriate wattage (usually between 15W to 50W for general electronics work).
    o **Tip Variety**: The tip of the soldering iron comes in different shapes (e.g., conical, chisel, or bevel) depending on the type of work you're doing. A fine-tipped soldering iron is ideal for small components, while a wider tip can be used for larger components or heavy-duty work.
2. **Solder**:

- The solder is a fusible metal used to form the connection. It typically consists of a mixture of **tin** and **lead**, although lead-free solder is now more common due to health concerns.
- **Wire Solder**: This is the most common type of solder, and it is often available in spools. The wire should have a core of flux, which helps the solder flow more easily and prevents oxidation.

3. **Soldering Iron Stand**:
   - The soldering iron stand holds your soldering iron when it's not in use. It is essential for safety and preventing accidental burns. Some stands have a cleaning sponge for cleaning the tip of the iron.

4. **Soldering Iron Tip Cleaner**:
   - To keep the tip of your soldering iron in good condition, you need to clean it regularly. This can be done using a damp sponge or a metal wire tip cleaner. Cleaning the tip helps maintain heat transfer efficiency.

5. **Tweezers**:
   - Fine-tipped tweezers are useful for holding small components in place while soldering, especially for surface-mount devices.

6. **Desoldering Pump**:

- o A desoldering pump is used to remove solder from connections, such as when you need to fix a mistake or remove a component. It works by sucking up molten solder after it's been heated by the soldering iron.

7. **Wire Cutters**:

- o Wire cutters are used to trim the excess leads of components after they have been soldered in place.

8. **Heat Shrink Tubing (Optional)**:

- o Heat shrink tubing is used to cover exposed wires or soldered connections, providing insulation and preventing shorts.

9. **Safety Glasses**:

- o Always wear safety glasses when soldering to protect your eyes from hot solder splashes and fumes.

10. **Soldering Mat**:

- o A heat-resistant mat provides a safe surface for soldering. It helps protect your workbench and provides a stable platform for your circuit.

Step-by-Step Guide to Soldering a Basic Circuit

Now that you have the necessary tools, let's walk through the basic steps of soldering a simple circuit.

Step 1: Prepare Your Workspace

- Set up a clean, well-lit, and well-ventilated workspace. Make sure all your tools are within reach and that you're working on a heat-resistant surface. Place a soldering mat under your work area to protect the surface from heat damage.

Step 2: Plug in the Soldering Iron

- Plug in the soldering iron and allow it to heat up. This can take a few minutes, depending on the wattage. Most soldering irons have an indicator light that turns off when the iron has reached the correct temperature (around 350°C or 660°F for general electronics soldering).

Step 3: Clean the Soldering Iron Tip

- Once the iron is heated, clean the tip by wiping it on a damp sponge or using a metal tip cleaner. This removes any old solder and prevents the tip from becoming corroded.

Step 4: Insert Components into the PCB

- Insert the leads of your components (resistors, capacitors, etc.) into the holes on the PCB. Make sure the component is seated properly, and bend the leads slightly to hold the components in place while soldering.

Step 5: Heat the Connection

- Place the tip of the soldering iron on the joint where the component lead and the PCB meet. Hold the soldering iron in place for about 1-2 seconds to heat the components evenly. Do not leave the iron in place for too long, as this can damage the components.

Step 6: Apply Solder

- While the components are heated, feed the solder wire into the joint. The solder should flow smoothly around the lead and the PCB pad. Once the joint is filled with solder, remove the solder and the soldering iron. The joint should look shiny and smooth. If the joint looks dull or cold, you may need to reflow it by heating it again and adding more solder.

Step 7: Trim the Leads

- Once the solder has cooled and solidified, use wire cutters to trim the excess leads from the components, leaving just a small amount of lead protruding from the PCB.

Step 8: Inspect the Solder Joints

- Inspect your solder joints to ensure they are solid. A good solder joint should be smooth, shiny, and cover both the component lead and the PCB pad. Avoid cold solder joints (dull and cracked) and solder bridges (unintended connections between pads).

Step 9: Clean the Solder Joints

- After soldering, you can clean the PCB using isopropyl alcohol and a soft brush to remove any flux residue. This will help prevent corrosion and ensure the circuit works properly.

Step 10: Test Your Circuit

- After you have finished soldering all the components, it's time to test your circuit. Power up the circuit and check for any issues like overheating, incorrect voltage, or malfunctioning components. If something isn't working, use a multimeter to check for bad connections or solder bridges.

Soldering is an essential skill for building and repairing electronic circuits. By following these steps and using the right tools, you can create strong, reliable connections for your projects. Practice is key to mastering soldering, so start with simple circuits and work your way up to more complex designs. With time, you'll become more confident and proficient at soldering and creating your own electronic creations.

CHAPTER 8

POWER SOURCES AND BATTERIES

Different Types of Power Sources

Power sources are essential for providing the electrical energy needed to run electronic circuits and devices. There are various types of power sources, each with specific characteristics that make them suitable for different applications. Understanding the different power sources is crucial for selecting the right one for your project.

Here are some of the most common types of power sources used in electronics:

1. **AC Power (Alternating Current)**:
   o AC power is the most common form of electricity used in homes and businesses. It is supplied by power companies through the electrical grid and is typically used to power large devices like household appliances, industrial equipment, and home electronics.

- o **Pros**: AC power can be easily transmitted over long distances, making it ideal for large-scale distribution. It's also more efficient for powering motors and certain types of equipment.

- o **Cons**: AC power must be converted to DC (direct current) for many electronics projects, as most circuits and devices require DC power to operate.

2. **DC Power (Direct Current)**:

- o DC power flows in one direction, and it is commonly used in battery-powered devices and most modern electronic circuits. Examples of DC power sources include batteries, power adapters, and DC power supplies.

- o **Pros**: DC power is stable and straightforward to use in electronics. It's used in most low-voltage applications, such as microcontrollers, sensors, and LEDs.

- o **Cons**: DC power is not as easy to transmit over long distances as AC power, and converting AC to DC can involve additional components like rectifiers.

3. **Batteries**:

- o Batteries are portable power sources that store electrical energy chemically and release it as needed. They come in various types, sizes, and voltages, making them suitable for different applications.

- o **Pros**: Batteries are compact, portable, and provide a self-contained power source. They are used in everything from flashlights to mobile phones and wearable devices.
- o **Cons**: Batteries have a limited lifespan and must be replaced or recharged after use. Their capacity depends on the type and size of the battery.

4. **Power Supplies**:

- o Power supplies are devices that convert AC power from the electrical grid into DC power that can be used by electronic circuits. They often feature adjustable voltage and current settings to provide the appropriate power for different components.
- o **Pros**: Power supplies are reliable and can deliver stable power for complex projects. They are commonly used in laboratory settings and for powering electronics prototypes.
- o **Cons**: Power supplies are usually not portable and are typically used in controlled environments where a steady power source is needed.

5. **Solar Power**:

- o Solar power is an eco-friendly option for providing DC power by converting sunlight into electricity using solar panels. It's commonly used in remote areas or in projects designed for sustainability.

- o **Pros**: Solar power is renewable and environmentally friendly. It can be used in outdoor or off-grid applications.
- o **Cons**: Solar power is intermittent and dependent on sunlight. It may require additional components like batteries for energy storage when sunlight is not available.

6. **Fuel Cells**:

- o Fuel cells generate electricity through a chemical reaction, typically by using hydrogen and oxygen. They are used in specialized applications like electric vehicles and backup power systems.
- o **Pros**: Fuel cells produce clean energy with water as the only byproduct, making them environmentally friendly.
- o **Cons**: Fuel cells are expensive and less commonly used in everyday electronics due to cost and infrastructure limitations.

How Batteries Work and Choosing the Right Battery for Your Project

Batteries are widely used to power electronics because they are portable and provide a stable power source. Understanding how batteries work and how to choose the right one for your project is crucial for ensuring that your device functions properly.

1. **How Batteries Work**:
   - A battery stores chemical energy that can be converted into electrical energy when needed. The basic components of a battery are the **anode** (negative terminal), **cathode** (positive terminal), and **electrolyte** (a substance that allows ions to move between the anode and cathode).
   - When the battery is connected to a circuit, a chemical reaction occurs that causes electrons to flow from the anode to the cathode through the external circuit, providing power to the device.
   - The voltage of a battery depends on the type of chemicals used in the battery. For example, a common AA battery provides 1.5 volts, while a typical lithium-ion battery provides around 3.7 volts.

2. **Types of Batteries**:
   - **Alkaline Batteries**: Alkaline batteries are widely used in household devices like remote controls, flashlights, and toys. They are inexpensive and

have a good shelf life, but their capacity is limited for high-drain applications.

o **Lithium-Ion Batteries**: Lithium-ion (Li-ion) batteries are rechargeable and commonly used in mobile phones, laptops, and electric vehicles. They have a high energy density and can deliver a consistent voltage over a long period. However, they require special charging circuits and should not be overcharged or discharged excessively.

o **Nickel-Metal Hydride (NiMH) Batteries**: NiMH batteries are commonly used in rechargeable applications and provide a good balance between cost and performance. They are often used in digital cameras, portable electronics, and power tools.

o **Lead-Acid Batteries**: Lead-acid batteries are typically used in larger applications such as backup power systems and automotive applications. They are inexpensive but heavy and have a shorter lifespan compared to other types of rechargeable batteries.

o **Coin-Cell Batteries**: Coin-cell batteries are small, flat batteries used in low-power devices like watches, hearing aids, and key fobs. They have a relatively low capacity but are perfect for devices that require minimal power.

3. **Choosing the Right Battery**:

  o **Voltage Requirements**: Ensure that the battery provides the correct voltage for your circuit. Some devices, like microcontrollers, require specific voltage levels (e.g., 3.3V, 5V).

  o **Capacity and Runtime**: The capacity of a battery, measured in milliamp-hours (mAh), determines how long the battery will last. Higher capacity batteries can power devices for longer periods but may be larger or heavier.

  o **Rechargeability**: If you need a battery that can be recharged, consider a rechargeable battery like a lithium-ion or NiMH battery. Rechargeable batteries are more cost-effective in the long run, but they may require a dedicated charging circuit.

  o **Size and Form Factor**: Make sure the battery fits within the physical space available in your device. Some devices may require specialized battery sizes or shapes (e.g., coin cells, or cylindrical cells).

Real-World Example: Powering a Portable Device

Let's consider powering a **portable Bluetooth speaker** as an example of how batteries are used in a real-world device. The speaker requires a power source that is compact, provides sufficient runtime, and is rechargeable. Here's how the battery choice and design come into play:

1. **Choosing the Battery**:

    o The Bluetooth speaker requires a voltage of 5V to power its internal electronics and speakers. A common choice for portable devices is a **Lithium-Ion (Li-ion)** rechargeable battery because it offers high energy density, is lightweight, and provides a stable voltage.

    o The battery capacity needs to be sufficient to provide hours of playback. A typical portable Bluetooth speaker might use a 3.7V 2200mAh Li-ion battery. This gives it a good balance of portability and runtime.

2. **Battery Charging**:

    o To recharge the battery, a **USB charging circuit** is included in the speaker. The USB port allows users to plug the speaker into a power adapter, and the charging circuit regulates the voltage and current to safely charge the battery.

    o The speaker may also include **overcharge protection** and **voltage regulation** to prevent damage to the battery during charging.

3. **Power Management**:

○ The speaker likely includes a **power management IC (PMIC)** that handles battery charging and power distribution to the internal circuits. This ensures that the battery is used efficiently, and the device can operate at peak performance while maintaining battery health.

By choosing the right battery and integrating power management components, the Bluetooth speaker can offer a long-lasting and portable power solution while keeping the device lightweight and compact.

In this chapter, you've learned about different types of power sources, how batteries work, and how to choose the right battery for your project. Whether you're designing a portable device or powering a complex circuit, understanding these fundamentals will help you make informed decisions and ensure your project runs smoothly.

CHAPTER 9

THE MAGIC OF INTEGRATED CIRCUITS (ICS)

What Are ICs and Why Are They Used?

An **Integrated Circuit (IC)** is a small electronic device made up of many components, such as transistors, resistors, capacitors, and diodes, all embedded into a single chip of semiconductor material (usually silicon). ICs are designed to perform specific functions, such as amplification, logic operations, signal processing, or power management.

ICs are used because they allow for the miniaturization of electronic devices. Before ICs, electronic circuits were built using individual components, which were larger, more expensive, and consumed more power. With ICs, many components are integrated onto a single chip, making the design more efficient and compact.

Why ICs are Important:

1. **Compactness**: ICs allow complex circuits to fit into small, space-efficient packages. This makes them ideal

for everything from microprocessors to communication devices, where space is a critical factor.

2. **Cost-Effectiveness**: Manufacturing ICs in bulk is less expensive compared to building circuits with individual components. This has led to reduced costs in consumer electronics and has made technology more accessible.

3. **Reliability**: ICs are more reliable than traditional circuits because the components are all built together and are less likely to fail due to external factors such as wiring problems or component loosening.

4. **Energy Efficiency**: ICs consume less power than discrete components because they are smaller and optimized for performance. This is especially important in battery-powered devices, like smartphones and wearables.

Overall, ICs have revolutionized electronics by enabling the creation of smaller, more powerful, and affordable devices that we use in our everyday lives.

Common Types of ICs in Electronics

There are many different types of ICs, each designed for a specific purpose in an electronic circuit. Some of the most common types of ICs include:

1. **Linear ICs**:

o **Definition**: Linear ICs are designed to amplify signals. They operate in a continuous range and are often used in audio, radio, and other analog applications.

o **Examples**:

- **Operational Amplifiers (Op-Amps)**: Used in signal processing, audio amplification, and active filters.

- **Voltage Regulators**: Used to maintain a stable output voltage regardless of input voltage fluctuations (e.g., 7805 for 5V regulation).

2. **Digital ICs**:

o **Definition**: Digital ICs handle discrete signals (0s and 1s), meaning they work with binary data. They are commonly used in logic circuits, computers, and microcontrollers.

o **Examples**:

- **Logic Gates (AND, OR, NOT)**: These are the building blocks for digital circuits and are used to perform basic logical operations.

- **Microcontrollers**: These are programmable ICs used in embedded systems to control various functions of a device (e.g., Arduino, ESP32).

- **Memory ICs**: Used to store data, such as **RAM** (Random Access Memory) and **ROM** (Read-Only Memory).

3. **Power ICs**:
    o **Definition**: Power ICs are used for power management, converting and regulating power in electronic devices.
    o **Examples**:
        - **DC-DC Converters**: These ICs convert one voltage level to another, for example, from 12V to 5V to power a microcontroller.
        - **Battery Chargers**: Used in portable devices to manage the charging of batteries and ensure safe operation.

4. **Radio-Frequency (RF) ICs**:
    o **Definition**: RF ICs are designed to work with high-frequency signals, such as those used in communication systems.
    o **Examples**:
        - **RF Amplifiers**: Used to amplify weak radio signals in communication systems like radios and wireless devices.
        - **Mixers and Oscillators**: Used in frequency conversion and signal modulation.

73

5. **Application-Specific ICs (ASICs)**:
   o **Definition**: ASICs are custom-designed ICs built to perform specific tasks, such as handling data compression or encryption.
   o **Examples**:
     ▪ **Graphics Processing Units (GPUs)**: Used in computers and gaming consoles to process visual data for rendering images and videos.

6. **System on a Chip (SoC)**:
   o **Definition**: An SoC is a more advanced type of IC that integrates an entire system, including a processor, memory, input/output interfaces, and more, onto a single chip.
   o **Examples**:
     ▪ **Smartphone SoCs**: Such as the Qualcomm Snapdragon or Apple A-series, which combine the CPU, GPU, and other components necessary for a smartphone's operation.

Example Project Using an IC

Let's look at a practical example of using an IC in a simple circuit. In this case, we'll use an **LM555 Timer IC**, which is a popular IC used for generating precise timing pulses, oscillations, or square waves.

Project: Building a Simple LED Flasher Circuit

In this project, we'll use the **LM555 timer** IC to create a simple LED flasher circuit. The 555 timer can be configured in astable mode to generate a square wave, which will blink an LED on and off at a regular interval.

Components:

- 555 Timer IC
- Resistor (e.g., 10kΩ)
- Capacitor (e.g., 100μF)
- LED
- Breadboard
- Jumper wires
- Power supply (e.g., 9V battery)

Steps:

1. **Insert the 555 Timer IC**: Place the 555 timer IC onto the breadboard. The IC has 8 pins, and we will use pins 4 (RESET), 8 (VCC), 1 (GND), 2 (TRIGGER), 3 (OUTPUT), 6 (THRESHOLD), 5 (CONTROL), and 7 (DISCHARGE).

2. **Connect Power**: Connect pin 8 (VCC) to the positive rail of the breadboard and pin 1 (GND) to the negative rail. Use a 9V battery or a DC power supply.

3. **Set up the Timing Components**:
   - Connect a **10kΩ resistor** between pins 7 (DISCHARGE) and 8 (VCC).
   - Connect a **100µF capacitor** between pins 6 (THRESHOLD) and 1 (GND).
   - Connect pin 2 (TRIGGER) to pin 6 (THRESHOLD).

4. **Connect the LED**: Connect the **LED** to pin 3 (OUTPUT) through a current-limiting resistor (e.g., 330Ω) and then to pin 1 (GND).

5. **Adjust the Frequency**: The frequency at which the LED blinks is determined by the resistor and capacitor values. In this case, the timing cycle will cause the LED to blink on and off, creating a visual signal.

6. **Power the Circuit**: Once everything is connected, power up the circuit by connecting the battery or DC power supply. The LED should blink on and off at a regular interval determined by the resistor and capacitor values.

This simple circuit demonstrates the magic of ICs, as the **555 timer** handles all the timing and logic required to blink the LED. The IC does all the work of generating the pulse, making it much easier to create this functionality without building the logic from scratch using transistors or other components.

In this chapter, you've learned about the importance of ICs in modern electronics, common types of ICs used in different applications, and how to use an IC in a simple circuit. Understanding ICs and their functionality is key to designing efficient and powerful electronic devices. With this knowledge, you can now incorporate ICs into your own projects to save space, reduce component count, and improve performance.

CHAPTER 10

UNDERSTANDING MICROCONTROLLERS

What Is a Microcontroller?

A **microcontroller** is a small, integrated circuit (IC) designed to perform specific tasks in embedded systems. It is essentially a mini-computer on a single chip, with a **central processing unit (CPU)**, memory, and input/output (I/O) ports, all integrated into one package. Microcontrollers are designed to interact with external devices, process data, and control various processes within electronic systems.

Unlike general-purpose computers that require an operating system and run multiple applications, microcontrollers are programmed to perform one or a few specific tasks. They are used in a wide range of devices, from household appliances to industrial machinery, providing control and automation for different applications.

Microcontrollers are often referred to as **embedded systems** because they are built into the device they control, making them different from general-purpose processors used in desktop computers.

Basic Architecture of a Microcontroller

The basic architecture of a microcontroller includes several key components that work together to perform its tasks. Here's a breakdown of these components:

1. **Central Processing Unit (CPU):**
   - The CPU is the brain of the microcontroller. It executes instructions stored in the program memory and controls the flow of data between the various components. It processes the inputs, performs calculations, and provides the output.
   - Most microcontrollers are based on a **Harvard architecture**, meaning they have separate memory spaces for program code and data. This allows for faster execution of instructions.

2. **Memory:**
   - **Program Memory (Flash Memory):** This is where the program code is stored. Flash memory is non-volatile, meaning it retains its contents even when the power is turned off. The program memory is typically used to store the firmware (the software that runs on the microcontroller).

o **RAM (Random Access Memory)**: RAM is used for temporary data storage while the microcontroller is running. It is volatile, meaning it loses its contents when the power is turned off. The microcontroller uses RAM to store variables, buffers, and temporary data during operation.

o **EEPROM (Electrically Erasable Programmable Read-Only Memory)**: This is a small amount of non-volatile memory used to store configuration settings or data that must persist after power-off, such as user settings.

3. **Input/Output (I/O) Ports**:

o I/O ports allow the microcontroller to interact with external devices. These ports can be configured as input or output depending on the needs of the application.

o **Digital I/O**: These pins can read or send digital signals (high or low voltage).

o **Analog I/O**: Some microcontrollers have analog-to-digital converters (ADC) and digital-to-analog converters (DAC), which allow the microcontroller to interact with analog signals (e.g., sensors that provide continuous voltage levels).

4. **Timers and Counters**:

- o Microcontrollers often include timers and counters to measure time or create delays. These are essential for generating clock pulses, controlling the timing of processes, or measuring the duration of events in the system.

5. **Serial Communication**:

- o Microcontrollers often include built-in communication interfaces such as **UART** (Universal Asynchronous Receiver-Transmitter), **SPI** (Serial Peripheral Interface), or **I2C** (Inter-Integrated Circuit) for communication with other devices like sensors, actuators, or other microcontrollers.

6. **Clock**:

- o The clock provides a timing reference for the microcontroller to synchronize operations. It is typically generated by a crystal oscillator or an internal clock source and controls the speed at which the microcontroller executes instructions.

7. **Watchdog Timer**:

- o A watchdog timer is a safety feature that resets the microcontroller if the system becomes unresponsive or enters an error state. It ensures that the system continues to operate properly by forcing a reset in case of failure.

How Microcontrollers Are Used in Everyday Gadgets

Microcontrollers are embedded in a vast array of everyday devices, helping to control and automate functions. Here are some common examples of how microcontrollers are used:

1. **Home Appliances**:
   - **Washing Machines**: Microcontrollers control the operation of washing machines, regulating water temperature, washing cycle time, and motor speed based on user settings. They may also have sensors to detect the water level or the type of laundry being washed.
   - **Microwave Ovens**: Microcontrollers in microwaves manage the timing of cooking cycles, adjust power levels, and handle keypad inputs from the user. They also ensure safety features like automatic turn-off after a certain time or if the door is opened.
   - **Refrigerators**: Microcontrollers control the temperature settings, monitor cooling cycles, and manage energy-saving modes in refrigerators. They can also be used in modern "smart" refrigerators with touchscreens and internet connectivity.
2. **Automobiles**:

- o **Engine Control Units (ECUs)**: Microcontrollers are widely used in vehicles to control the engine's operation, manage fuel injection, monitor exhaust systems, and ensure the vehicle runs efficiently. They also handle tasks like controlling airbag deployment or regulating cruise control.
- o **Infotainment Systems**: In modern cars, microcontrollers are used to manage touch screens, audio systems, navigation, and connectivity features like Bluetooth and Wi-Fi.

3. **Wearable Devices**:

- o **Smartwatches**: Microcontrollers are at the heart of smartwatches, managing the display, processing user input (touchscreen or buttons), controlling sensors (heart rate monitors, accelerometers), and connecting to other devices like smartphones via Bluetooth.
- o **Fitness Trackers**: Similar to smartwatches, microcontrollers in fitness trackers monitor activity, store data, and communicate with smartphones to sync data like steps, calories burned, or heart rate.

4. **Toys and Entertainment Devices**:

- o **Remote-Controlled Toys**: Microcontrollers are used in toys to control motors, sensors, and communication systems. They allow the toy to move, respond to commands, and even interact with the environment.

- o **Video Game Consoles**: Microcontrollers in video game consoles help manage inputs from controllers, display output on screens, and handle complex audio and video processing tasks.

5. **Smart Devices**:

- o **Smart Thermostats**: Microcontrollers regulate the temperature in smart thermostats by receiving input from temperature sensors and controlling the heating or cooling system accordingly. They can also be controlled remotely through smartphones, allowing for automated temperature adjustments.

- o **Smart Lights**: Microcontrollers control the operation of smart light bulbs, enabling features like dimming, color-changing, and scheduling through mobile apps or voice assistants (e.g., Amazon Alexa, Google Assistant).

6. **Medical Devices**:

- o **Blood Glucose Monitors**: Microcontrollers are used in medical devices like blood glucose monitors, where they collect data from sensors, process the information, and provide results to the user through a display or mobile app.

o **Hearing Aids**: Modern hearing aids often rely on microcontrollers to process sound signals, adjust volume levels, and filter background noise for improved hearing.

Conclusion

Microcontrollers are powerful, versatile components used in a wide variety of everyday devices. They provide control, automation, and intelligence to everything from household appliances to medical devices and wearable technology. By understanding the basic architecture of microcontrollers and how they are used, you can begin to explore their applications in your own projects, whether for creating a new gadget or enhancing an existing one. As technology continues to advance, the role of microcontrollers in our daily lives will only continue to grow.

CHAPTER 11

PROGRAMMING FOR MICROCONTROLLERS

Basics of Programming Languages for Microcontrollers

Programming microcontrollers involves writing code that enables the microcontroller to interact with its environment by reading inputs, performing computations, and controlling outputs. The code written for a microcontroller must be efficient, reliable, and work within the constraints of the microcontroller's processing power, memory, and I/O capabilities.

Here are some common programming languages used for microcontrollers:

1. **C and C++**:
   - C and C++ are the most commonly used programming languages for microcontrollers. These languages provide a good balance of low-level control over hardware and high-level features, making them ideal for embedded systems.

- o **Why Use C/C++?**:
  - **Portability**: C/C++ code can be used across different microcontroller platforms, though it may need slight adjustments based on the hardware.
  - **Efficiency**: These languages allow for direct manipulation of memory and hardware registers, making them ideal for resource-constrained environments like microcontrollers.
  - **Widely Supported**: Most microcontroller manufacturers provide C or C++ compilers and libraries tailored to their devices.

2. **Assembly Language**:
   - o Assembly language is a low-level programming language that is closely tied to the microcontroller's instruction set. It is used for time-critical applications where direct hardware control is required.
   - o **Why Use Assembly?**:
     - **Optimized Performance**: Assembly code can be highly optimized for speed and size, making it ideal for embedded systems with strict performance requirements.

- **Control**: Assembly provides precise control over the hardware, making it useful for applications like real-time systems and embedded applications where low-level programming is crucial.
  - **Challenges**: Writing in assembly is time-consuming and difficult to maintain, which is why it's typically used only for very specific tasks.

3. **Python**:
   - Some microcontrollers, especially **Raspberry Pi** and **micro:bit**, support Python, a high-level language that is easier for beginners to learn.
   - **Why Use Python?**:
     - **Ease of Use**: Python has a simple syntax, making it a good choice for beginners.
     - **Libraries**: Python supports a rich set of libraries for interfacing with sensors, displays, and other peripherals.

4. **Arduino Programming Language**:
   - The Arduino platform simplifies the process of programming microcontrollers. While the Arduino IDE uses C/C++ under the hood, it provides an easy-to-understand, simplified interface that lets beginners write code more quickly.

- o **Why Use Arduino?**:
  - **Beginner-Friendly**: The Arduino IDE and its libraries provide a simple environment for beginners to get started with microcontroller programming.
  - **Large Community**: Arduino has a large online community with plenty of resources, tutorials, and examples, making it easier to find support.

Example: Writing a Simple Program to Blink an LED

One of the simplest and most common microcontroller projects is writing a program to blink an LED on and off. This demonstrates how a microcontroller can control outputs and interact with the physical world.

Let's create a simple program for an **Arduino microcontroller** to blink an LED.

Components Needed:

- Arduino board (e.g., Arduino Uno)
- LED
- 220Ω resistor
- Breadboard and jumper wires

Steps:

1. **Connect the Circuit**:
   - Insert the **LED** into the breadboard with the longer leg (anode) connected to digital pin 13 on the Arduino, and the shorter leg (cathode) connected to one side of the resistor.
   - Connect the other side of the resistor to **GND** (ground) on the Arduino.

2. **Write the Code**: Open the **Arduino IDE** (more on this in the next section), and write the following program:

cpp

```cpp
// Define pin for LED
const int ledPin = 13;   // LED connected to
digital pin 13

void setup() {
  // Initialize the digital pin as an output
  pinMode(ledPin, OUTPUT);
}

void loop() {
  // Turn the LED on
  digitalWrite(ledPin, HIGH);
  // Wait for 1000 milliseconds (1 second)
```

```
delay(1000);
// Turn the LED off
digitalWrite(ledPin, LOW);
// Wait for 1000 milliseconds (1 second)
delay(1000);
}
```

Explanation:

- The `pinMode()` function sets **pin 13** as an output pin, which will control the LED.
- The `digitalWrite()` function is used to set the pin HIGH (on) or LOW (off), which controls the LED's state.
- The `delay()` function pauses the program for the specified number of milliseconds (1000 ms = 1 second) between turning the LED on and off.

3. **Upload the Program**:
    o Connect the Arduino board to your computer via a USB cable.
    o Select the appropriate board and port in the **Tools** menu of the Arduino IDE.
    o Click the **Upload** button in the Arduino IDE to upload the program to the Arduino.
4. **Observe the LED**:
    o Once the code is uploaded, you should see the LED blinking on and off every second.

This simple program is an excellent way to start learning how to program a microcontroller. It teaches you how to use basic functions like pin initialization, output control, and timing.

How to Use Development Environments (e.g., Arduino IDE)

A development environment, or **IDE (Integrated Development Environment)**, is where you write, edit, and upload your code to a microcontroller. For beginners, the **Arduino IDE** is one of the most user-friendly environments available for microcontroller programming.

1. **Installing the Arduino IDE**:
   - o Download the **Arduino IDE** from the official Arduino website (https://www.arduino.cc/en/software).
   - o Install the IDE on your computer by following the installation instructions for your operating system.
2. **Setting Up the IDE**:
   - o After installation, open the Arduino IDE. The IDE provides a simple text editor for writing code and buttons to compile and upload the code to the microcontroller.

o Connect your Arduino board to your computer via USB and select the correct board and port from the **Tools** menu.

3. **Writing Code in the Arduino IDE**:

   o The Arduino IDE uses a simplified version of C/C++ programming, which is made easy by a set of built-in functions and libraries.

   o The main structure of an Arduino program consists of two functions:

      ▪ `setup()`: Runs once when the program starts and is used to initialize settings.

      ▪ `loop()`: Repeats continuously after `setup()` and runs the main logic of the program.

4. **Compiling and Uploading Code**:

   o After writing your code, click the **Verify** button (checkmark) to compile the code and check for errors.

   o Once the code is compiled successfully, click the **Upload** button (right arrow) to send the code to the Arduino board.

5. **Using Libraries**:

   o The Arduino IDE provides built-in libraries for common tasks such as controlling motors, using sensors, or displaying information on an LCD.

You can include these libraries in your programs to simplify coding.

- To use a library, go to **Sketch** → **Include Library** and select the library you need.

6. **Serial Monitor**:

- The **Serial Monitor** in the Arduino IDE allows you to communicate with the Arduino board via the USB connection. You can use it to send data to the board or display output from the microcontroller (e.g., sensor readings or debugging information).

Conclusion

In this chapter, you've learned the basics of programming microcontrollers, including the most common programming languages used, the structure of microcontroller code, and how to create a simple program to blink an LED. The Arduino IDE serves as an excellent tool for beginners, allowing you to quickly write, compile, and upload code to your microcontroller. Whether you are building a simple project or developing a more complex system, mastering microcontroller programming is a key skill for creating interactive electronic devices.

CHAPTER 12

SENSORS AND THEIR APPLICATIONS

Types of Sensors (Temperature, Motion, Light)

Sensors are essential components that allow microcontrollers and electronic systems to interact with the physical world. They detect changes in the environment and convert these changes into electrical signals that can be processed by the microcontroller. Sensors come in various types, each designed to measure specific physical properties. Below are three common types of sensors:

1. **Temperature Sensors**:
   - **Function**: Temperature sensors measure the temperature of an environment or object. These sensors are critical in applications where maintaining a specific temperature is important, such as in climate control systems or appliances.
   - **Types**:
     - **Thermistors**: These are resistors whose resistance changes significantly with

temperature. They are commonly used in temperature sensing applications.

- **Thermocouples**: A thermocouple is made of two different metal wires that produce a voltage based on the temperature difference between their junctions. Thermocouples are widely used in industrial applications due to their wide temperature range.

- **LM35**: This is an example of a popular temperature sensor that outputs an analog voltage proportional to the temperature in Celsius. It's often used with microcontrollers like Arduino.

2. **Motion Sensors**:

  o **Function**: Motion sensors detect movement within a defined range. These sensors are used in security systems, automatic lighting systems, and motion detection devices.

  o **Types**:

    - **PIR (Passive Infrared) Sensors**: These sensors detect infrared radiation (heat) emitted by objects. They are commonly used for detecting human presence or movement in security systems and automatic lighting.

- **Ultrasonic Sensors**: Ultrasonic sensors send out high-frequency sound waves and measure the time it takes for the waves to bounce back. The time delay gives information about the distance to an object, which can be used to detect movement or measure proximity.

- **Accelerometers**: These sensors measure acceleration or movement in a specific direction. They are used in devices like smartphones, fitness trackers, and gaming controllers.

3. **Light Sensors**:

   o **Function**: Light sensors detect the intensity of light in an environment. These sensors are used in devices that need to respond to changes in lighting conditions, such as automatic brightness adjustment or light-based security systems.

   o **Types**:

     - **LDR (Light Dependent Resistor)**: An LDR is a resistor whose resistance decreases as light intensity increases. LDRs are commonly used for automatic lighting or light detection circuits.

     - **Photodiodes**: These are semiconductor devices that generate a current when exposed to light. They are often used in applications like light meters, cameras, and optical systems.

- **Phototransistors**: Similar to photodiodes, phototransistors can amplify the current generated by light exposure, making them useful in applications requiring higher sensitivity.

Real-World Examples of Sensors in Devices Like Smartphones and Thermostats

Sensors are integrated into many modern devices to make them interactive and responsive to the environment. Below are some real-world examples of sensors and their applications in everyday gadgets:

1. **Smartphones**:
   - **Accelerometer**: An accelerometer in a smartphone detects the orientation and motion of the phone. It enables features like screen rotation (landscape/portrait mode) and step tracking in fitness apps.
   - **Gyroscope**: A gyroscope is used in combination with the accelerometer to improve motion sensing accuracy. It helps stabilize image and

video capture, especially in apps that use augmented reality (AR).

o **Proximity Sensor**: Proximity sensors detect when the phone is near your face, which helps disable the touchscreen during phone calls to prevent accidental touches.

o **Ambient Light Sensor**: This sensor adjusts the brightness of the phone's display based on the surrounding light, providing better visibility in bright environments and conserving battery in darker settings.

2. **Thermostats**:

o **Temperature Sensor**: Thermostats use temperature sensors (like thermistors or the LM35) to monitor the room's temperature. Based on the temperature readings, the thermostat controls heating or cooling systems to maintain the desired temperature.

o **Humidity Sensor**: In some smart thermostats, humidity sensors are used to monitor the moisture level in the air. This data is then used to adjust the environment for comfort, particularly in humid or dry climates.

o **Motion Sensor**: In smart thermostats, motion sensors (such as PIR sensors) are used to detect the presence of people in a room. If no motion is detected, the system may lower the temperature to save energy.

3. **Security Systems**:

    o   **PIR Motion Sensors**: In home security systems, PIR sensors detect motion in a room or area and trigger alarms or cameras to record footage when an intruder is detected.

    o   **Door/Window Sensors**: These sensors use magnetic switches to detect when a door or window is opened. They can trigger an alert to notify users of unauthorized access.

4. **Smart Lighting**:

    o   **LDR Light Sensors**: Smart lighting systems use LDR sensors to automatically adjust the brightness of lights depending on the ambient light. For example, lights can dim when it's bright outside and brighten when the sun sets.

    o   **Motion Sensors**: Used in smart lighting, these sensors detect the presence of people and turn lights on or off based on movement, often used in hallways, bathrooms, or outdoor lights.

How Sensors Are Interfaced with Microcontrollers

Microcontrollers are the "brains" of many sensor-based systems, taking inputs from sensors and processing them to control outputs (like turning on a fan or activating an alarm). Sensors typically provide data in one of two formats: **analog** or **digital**. Here's how sensors are interfaced with microcontrollers:

1. **Interfacing Analog Sensors**:
    - **Analog sensors**, like temperature sensors (e.g., LM35) and light-dependent resistors (LDRs), output a variable voltage that is proportional to the measured quantity (temperature, light intensity, etc.).
    - To interface an analog sensor with a microcontroller, you need to connect the sensor's output to one of the microcontroller's **analog-to-digital converter (ADC)** pins. The ADC converts the analog voltage into a digital value that the microcontroller can process.
    - Example: In a temperature sensor like the LM35, the voltage output increases by 10mV per degree Celsius. The microcontroller reads the voltage, converts it into a digital value, and uses that to control a heater or cooling system.

2. **Interfacing Digital Sensors**:
    - **Digital sensors**, such as motion sensors (PIR) or digital light sensors, output a binary signal—

either HIGH (1) or LOW (0)—indicating the presence or absence of a specific condition.

o These sensors are connected directly to the microcontroller's **digital I/O pins**, and the microcontroller can read the signal using simple digital read commands (`digitalRead()` in Arduino).

o Example: A PIR motion sensor outputs a HIGH signal when motion is detected. The microcontroller can then trigger an alarm or turn on a light based on the sensor's output.

3. **Using Sensor Libraries**:

o Many sensors come with **pre-written libraries** that simplify interfacing with microcontrollers. These libraries include functions for reading sensor data, calibrating the sensor, and processing the input.

o For example, the **DHT11** or **DHT22** sensor libraries allow you to easily read temperature and humidity data from the sensor without manually coding the sensor's communication protocol.

4. **Powering Sensors**:

o Some sensors require **external power** to function, such as 3.3V or 5V from the microcontroller's power pin or an external power supply. Make sure to check the power requirements of each sensor to ensure proper operation.

Example: Interfacing a Temperature Sensor with an Arduino

Let's look at a simple example where we use an LM35 temperature sensor with an **Arduino** to read the temperature and display it on the Serial Monitor.

Components Needed:

- Arduino (e.g., Arduino Uno)
- LM35 temperature sensor
- Breadboard and jumper wires

Steps:

1. **Connect the Sensor**:
   - Connect the **VCC** pin of the LM35 to the **5V** pin on the Arduino.
   - Connect the **GND** pin of the LM35 to the **GND** pin on the Arduino.
   - Connect the **output** pin of the LM35 to the **A0** analog input pin on the Arduino.
2. **Write the Code**:

cpp

```cpp
// Define the analog input pin
const int tempPin = A0;

void setup() {
  // Start serial communication at 9600 baud rate
  Serial.begin(9600);
}

void loop() {
  // Read the analog value from the temperature
sensor
  int sensorValue = analogRead(tempPin);

  // Convert the analog value to voltage (since
5V is the reference voltage)
  float voltage = sensorValue * (5.0 / 1023.0);

  // Convert the voltage to temperature in
Celsius (LM35 provides 10mV per degree)
  float temperature = voltage * 100.0;

  // Print the temperature to the Serial Monitor
  Serial.print("Temperature: ");
  Serial.print(temperature);
  Serial.println(" °C");

  // Wait for 1 second before reading again
```

```
delay(1000);
}
```

Explanation:

- The Arduino reads the analog signal from the LM35 sensor using `analogRead()`.
- The analog value is converted into a voltage, which is then used to calculate the temperature in Celsius.
- The result is displayed on the Serial Monitor.

3. **Upload and Test**:
    o   Upload the code to the Arduino board, and open the Serial Monitor to see the temperature readings from the LM35 sensor.

In this chapter, you've learned about different types of sensors (temperature, motion, and light), their applications in everyday devices, and how to interface them with microcontrollers. By understanding sensor functionality and using microcontrollers to process sensor data, you can create intelligent systems that respond to real-world conditions.

CHAPTER 13

UNDERSTANDING ACTUATORS

What Are Actuators and Their Role in Electronics?

An **actuator** is a device that converts electrical energy into physical movement. Actuators play a critical role in electronics by enabling microcontrollers and other control systems to perform physical tasks, such as moving, lifting, or rotating objects. They are often used in robotics, automation systems, HVAC (heating, ventilation, and air conditioning) controls, and many other applications where movement or mechanical action is required.

In essence, actuators are the "muscles" of an electronic system. They take the signals from microcontrollers (which typically handle logic and decision-making) and transform them into mechanical action, like turning a wheel, opening a valve, or positioning a part. Actuators can operate based on digital signals (on/off), analog signals (varying speed or position), or more complex control systems.

Actuators are used in many devices and systems, including **robotic arms**, **automated machinery**, **electric vehicles**,

home automation, and even in **medical devices** like ventilators and prosthetics.

Types of Actuators: Motors, Servos, and Solenoids

There are several types of actuators, and each is used in different applications based on the specific movement required. Below are some of the most common types:

1. **Motors**:
   - **Function**: Motors are perhaps the most common type of actuator. They convert electrical energy into rotary motion, which can be used to drive wheels, gears, fans, pumps, and other machinery.
   - **Types of Motors**:
     - **DC Motors**: A direct current (DC) motor is the simplest type of motor, providing continuous rotational motion when powered by a DC voltage. It is commonly used in small devices like toys, fans, or small robots.
     - **Stepper Motors**: Stepper motors rotate in discrete steps, making them ideal for applications requiring precise control of movement. They are commonly used in 3D printers, CNC machines, and camera

systems where fine positional control is needed.

- **AC Motors**: Alternating current (AC) motors use AC power to generate rotational motion. They are typically used in industrial machinery and large appliances, such as washing machines or air conditioners.

2. **Servos**:

  o **Function**: A servo is a special type of motor that is designed for precise control of angular position. Unlike regular motors, servos can rotate to specific angles and hold that position under load. This makes them ideal for applications where precise movement is needed, such as in robotics, model airplanes, or camera systems.

  o **How Servos Work**: A servo motor typically has a built-in feedback mechanism (usually a potentiometer) that continuously adjusts the motor's position. The servo receives a pulse-width modulation (PWM) signal, which controls the motor's position by determining how long the signal is high or low.

  o **Types of Servos**:

- **Standard Servo**: Used for applications where a range of motion (typically 0 to 180 degrees) is required.
- **Continuous Servo**: These servos do not have a fixed range of motion and can rotate continuously in either direction, making them ideal for driving wheels in mobile robots.

3. **Solenoids**:

- **Function**: A solenoid is a linear actuator that generates motion along a straight line, usually by using an electromagnet to pull or push a movable plunger. Solenoids are often used in applications like locks, valves, and pneumatic systems.

- **How Solenoids Work**: When current flows through the coil of a solenoid, it generates a magnetic field that pulls a metal plunger into the coil. When the current is switched off, a spring typically returns the plunger to its original position.

- **Applications**: Solenoids are commonly found in devices like **door locks, electromagnetic valves**, and **relays**. They are used for on/off switching or triggering specific actions, such as unlocking doors or actuating mechanical levers.

Example: Using a Motor to Control Movement in Robotics

In robotics, motors are often used to provide movement, whether it's for wheels, arms, or other mechanisms. For example, let's consider a simple **robotic car** powered by DC motors. The car can move forward, backward, or turn, depending on how the motors are controlled.

Let's walk through how motors can be used to control movement in a simple robotic project.

Components:

- Microcontroller (e.g., Arduino)
- 2 DC motors
- Motor driver (e.g., L298N or L293D)
- Chassis with wheels
- Battery pack
- Jumper wires

Steps:

1. **Wiring the Motors**:
   - Connect the two DC motors to the motor driver's output pins. The motor driver will control the

direction and speed of the motors based on the signals it receives from the microcontroller.

- o Connect the motor driver's input pins to the microcontroller (e.g., Arduino). These input pins will receive PWM signals to control the speed and direction of the motors.

- o Connect the motor driver's power input to the battery pack, as the motors require higher voltage than the microcontroller can provide.

2. **Programming the Microcontroller**:

- o Write a program for the microcontroller to control the motors. The program will send digital signals to the motor driver to control the direction of the motors and use PWM to adjust their speed.

Here's a simple Arduino code example to make the robot move forward, backward, and turn:

cpp

```cpp
// Define the motor pins
const int motorA1 = 3;
const int motorA2 = 4;
const int motorB1 = 5;
const int motorB2 = 6;

void setup() {
  // Set motor pins as output
```

```
  pinMode(motorA1, OUTPUT);
  pinMode(motorA2, OUTPUT);
  pinMode(motorB1, OUTPUT);
  pinMode(motorB2, OUTPUT);
}

void loop() {
  // Move forward
  digitalWrite(motorA1, HIGH);
  digitalWrite(motorA2, LOW);
  digitalWrite(motorB1, HIGH);
  digitalWrite(motorB2, LOW);
  delay(2000);  // Move forward for 2 seconds

  // Stop
  digitalWrite(motorA1, LOW);
  digitalWrite(motorA2, LOW);
  digitalWrite(motorB1, LOW);
  digitalWrite(motorB2, LOW);
  delay(1000);  // Stop for 1 second

  // Move backward
  digitalWrite(motorA1, LOW);
  digitalWrite(motorA2, HIGH);
  digitalWrite(motorB1, LOW);
  digitalWrite(motorB2, HIGH);
  delay(2000);  // Move backward for 2 seconds

  // Turn left
```

```
digitalWrite(motorA1, HIGH);
digitalWrite(motorA2, LOW);
digitalWrite(motorB1, LOW);
digitalWrite(motorB2, HIGH);
delay(1000);  // Turn left for 1 second

// Stop
digitalWrite(motorA1, LOW);
digitalWrite(motorA2, LOW);
digitalWrite(motorB1, LOW);
digitalWrite(motorB2, LOW);
delay(1000);  // Stop for 1 second
}
```

Explanation:

- The program sends signals to the motor driver to control the direction of the motors.
- The HIGH and LOW signals define the direction: one motor moves forward, and the other moves backward for forward movement, while reversing the direction of the motors causes the robot to move backward.
- The delay times determine how long the robot moves in each direction.

3. **Testing the Robot**:
   o After uploading the program to the Arduino, power up the system. The robot should move

forward, then stop, move backward, stop again, and finally turn left. This simple example demonstrates how motors control the movement of a robotic system.

Conclusion

Actuators, including motors, servos, and solenoids, are essential for translating electronic signals into physical movement. Motors are commonly used in robotics and automation, while servos offer precise control over angles, and solenoids are used for linear motion. Understanding how these actuators work and how to interface them with microcontrollers opens the door to creating interactive and dynamic systems, whether for hobbyist projects, industrial automation, or robotics.

CHAPTER 14

COMMUNICATION IN ELECTRONICS: WIRES, SIGNALS, AND PROTOCOLS

Basic Communication in Circuits

In electronics, **communication** refers to the transmission of data or signals between components or systems. This communication can occur in different forms, such as sending binary data, analog signals, or control commands between devices. Proper communication ensures that electronic systems work in harmony and perform the desired tasks.

Communication in circuits can involve multiple devices or parts of a system exchanging information, whether within a single microcontroller, between a microcontroller and sensors, or between different microcontroller-based systems. The information sent through a circuit can be either **digital** (represented by discrete 1s and 0s) or **analog** (represented by continuous signals).

Basic communication methods include:

115

- **Direct Wiring**: For simple circuits, components can be directly connected to each other via wires, where data flows through the wire as electrical signals.
- **Signal Modulation**: For long-distance communication, the signal may need to be modulated, or altered, to improve transmission or to encode the data.

Serial vs Parallel Communication

Two primary communication methods in circuits are **serial communication** and **parallel communication**. Both methods describe how data is transmitted between devices or components, but they differ in how data is transmitted over the communication lines.

1. **Serial Communication**:
   - **Definition**: In serial communication, data is transmitted bit by bit over a single communication line or wire. Bits are sent sequentially, one after another.
   - **Advantages**:
     - **Fewer Wires**: Serial communication requires fewer wires or connections, making it simpler and more cost-effective for long-distance communication.

- **Longer Distance**: Serial communication can work over greater distances without significant signal degradation.
- **Simplicity**: Fewer wires mean less complexity in circuit design, making it ideal for systems with multiple components or those with limited space.

○ **Disadvantages**:

- **Slower Data Transfer**: Because data is sent one bit at a time, serial communication is typically slower than parallel communication for transmitting large volumes of data.

○ **Examples**: Serial communication is used in protocols like **RS-232**, **USB**, and the popular **UART** (Universal Asynchronous Receiver-Transmitter) protocol.

2. **Parallel Communication**:

○ **Definition**: In parallel communication, multiple bits are transmitted simultaneously across multiple wires. Each wire carries one bit of the data at the same time.

○ **Advantages**:

- **Faster Data Transfer**: Because multiple bits are transmitted simultaneously, parallel communication can transfer data more quickly than serial communication.

- **Efficient for Short Distances**: Parallel communication is highly efficient for short-distance communication, such as between components on a microcontroller or on a computer motherboard.

o **Disadvantages**:

- **More Wires**: It requires more wiring, which can increase complexity, especially in systems with many components.

- **Signal Integrity Issues**: Over long distances, parallel communication can suffer from **signal degradation** and **crosstalk** between the wires, which can cause data corruption.

o **Examples**: Parallel communication is used in older computer interfaces like **printer ports** (IEEE 1284) and **internal computer buses**.

Common Protocols: SPI, I2C, UART

In modern electronics, various **communication protocols** are used to standardize the way devices exchange data. These protocols define the rules for how data is transmitted, ensuring that devices can correctly interpret the data sent and received. Some of the most common communication protocols in embedded systems and microcontroller applications include **SPI**, **I2C**, and **UART**.

1. **SPI (Serial Peripheral Interface)**:
   - **Definition**: SPI is a synchronous serial communication protocol used to transfer data between a master device (such as a microcontroller) and one or more peripheral devices (like sensors or displays).
   - **How It Works**:
     - SPI uses four signal lines: **MISO** (Master In Slave Out), **MOSI** (Master Out Slave In), **SCK** (Serial Clock), and **SS** (Slave Select).
     - The master device generates the clock signal (**SCK**), which synchronizes the data transfer. Data is transmitted one bit at a time, with each bit being clocked in by the master.
   - **Advantages**:
     - **Fast Data Transfer**: SPI supports high-speed data transfer, making it suitable for high-performance applications.

- **Full-Duplex**: Data can be transmitted and received simultaneously, allowing for faster communication.
- **Multiple Devices**: SPI can support multiple peripheral devices with separate chip select lines for each device.

o **Disadvantages**:

- **More Wires**: It requires at least four wires (plus one for each additional device) to operate, which can be inconvenient in systems with many peripherals.

2. **I2C (Inter-Integrated Circuit)**:

o **Definition**: I2C is a synchronous serial communication protocol that allows multiple devices to communicate over just two wires: **SCL** (Serial Clock) and **SDA** (Serial Data).

o **How It Works**:

- I2C uses a **master-slave** configuration. The master controls the clock and sends signals to the slaves to initiate communication.
- Each device on the I2C bus has a unique address, allowing the master to address a specific device to read from or write to.

o **Advantages**:

120

- **Fewer Wires**: I2C only requires two wires (clock and data), making it very simple for communication between multiple devices on a shared bus.
- **Multiple Devices**: I2C can support many devices on the same bus, with each device having a unique address.

○ **Disadvantages**:

- **Slower Speed**: I2C is slower than SPI, with typical speeds ranging from 100kHz to 400kHz (though higher speeds are possible).
- **Shared Bus**: All devices share the same bus, which can limit the maximum distance and number of devices in the system.

3. **UART (Universal Asynchronous Receiver-Transmitter)**:

○ **Definition**: UART is an asynchronous serial communication protocol commonly used for communication between two devices. It is one of the simplest protocols and requires only two wires: **TX** (Transmit) and **RX** (Receive).

○ **How It Works**:

- UART communication does not require a clock signal. Data is transmitted asynchronously, meaning there's no shared clock between the sender and receiver. The data is sent with start and stop bits to mark the beginning and end of each byte.

- The baud rate (the speed of data transmission) must be set to the same value on both communicating devices.

o **Advantages**:

- **Simple Wiring**: UART only requires two wires for communication, making it easy to implement in simple systems.

- **Widely Supported**: UART is widely used in communication between microcontrollers, sensors, GPS modules, and other serial devices.

o **Disadvantages**:

- **Slower Data Transfer**: UART is typically slower than SPI and I2C, with baud rates commonly ranging from 9600 to 115200 bps (bits per second).

- **Limited to Two Devices**: UART is typically used for point-to-point communication (one-to-one communication between devices), unlike

122

I2C or SPI, which can support multiple devices.

Conclusion

In this chapter, we've explored the basics of communication in electronic circuits, focusing on **serial** and **parallel communication** methods. We also delved into three common communication protocols—**SPI**, **I2C**, and **UART**—each with its own advantages and use cases. Understanding these communication protocols is essential for building complex electronic systems where multiple devices need to interact with one another. Whether you are working on a small project with a few sensors or a larger system with many interconnected components, knowing how to choose and implement the right protocol will ensure smooth and efficient communication between your devices.

CHAPTER 15

BUILDING YOUR FIRST SIMPLE CIRCUIT

Hands-On Project: Building a Simple LED Circuit

In this chapter, we'll walk through the process of building a simple LED circuit. This project is ideal for beginners and will help you understand how to connect components, use basic tools, and learn the fundamentals of circuit behavior.

Objective: Create a circuit that turns on an LED using a resistor to limit the current and protect the LED from damage.

Components Needed:

- 1 LED (Light Emitting Diode)
- 1 Resistor (typically 220Ω to 330Ω)
- 1 Breadboard (optional but recommended for prototyping)
- Jumper wires
- Power source (e.g., 5V DC power supply or a 9V battery with a connector)

- Microcontroller (optional, like an Arduino, for controlling the circuit, or you can use a direct connection to the power source for a simple setup)

Steps:

1. **Understanding the LED**:
   - An LED has two terminals: the **anode** (positive, longer lead) and the **cathode** (negative, shorter lead).
   - The current flows from the anode to the cathode when the LED is lit.

2. **Connect the Resistor**:
   - Connect one leg of the resistor to the **anode** of the LED. The purpose of the resistor is to limit the current flowing through the LED, preventing it from burning out.
   - The resistor is necessary because LEDs typically need a controlled amount of current (e.g., 20mA), and without a resistor, the current could exceed the LED's rating.

3. **Wire the LED to Power**:
   - Connect the other leg of the resistor to the **positive terminal (VCC)** of the power supply (usually 5V for small circuits).
   - Connect the **cathode** of the LED to the **negative terminal (GND)** of the power supply.

4. **Test the Circuit**:
   - o   If the power is connected correctly, the LED should light up. If it doesn't, check the connections and make sure the power supply is working.

5. **Using a Breadboard**:
   - o   If you are using a breadboard, insert the LED and resistor into the appropriate rows, making sure the connections are secure. The breadboard will allow you to quickly and easily modify or extend the circuit.

How to Test and Troubleshoot the Circuit

Troubleshooting is an essential skill when working with electronics. When a circuit doesn't work as expected, it's important to follow a systematic approach to identify and resolve the issue.

Here are some steps to help you test and troubleshoot your LED circuit:

1. **Check the Power Supply**:
   - o   Make sure the power supply is connected properly. Verify that the voltage is within the

appropriate range for your circuit (e.g., 5V or 9V, depending on your components).

- o If you're using a battery, check the battery's charge level.

2. **Verify Component Orientation**:

- o LEDs are polarity-sensitive, so make sure the **anode** (longer lead) is connected to the positive terminal and the **cathode** (shorter lead) is connected to the negative terminal.
- o If the LED is installed incorrectly, it won't light up.

3. **Inspect the Resistor**:

- o Ensure the resistor is connected in series with the LED to limit current. If the resistor is omitted or incorrectly placed, the LED may receive too much current and burn out, or it may not work at all.
- o Check the resistor's value to ensure it is appropriate for the LED. If you're unsure, a 220Ω or 330Ω resistor is a safe starting point for most small LEDs.

4. **Check for Loose Connections**:

- o Loose wires or poor connections are a common problem. If you're using a breadboard, ensure the components are securely connected and the wires are firmly seated in the breadboard's holes.

o If you're using jumper wires, make sure the ends are fully inserted into the breadboard or microcontroller headers.

5. **Use a Multimeter**:

o A multimeter can be used to test the voltage across the LED and resistor. Set the multimeter to measure DC voltage and check the circuit's voltage between the LED's anode and cathode.

o If you see a voltage drop across the LED, it indicates that the circuit is working. If there's no voltage or the voltage is too high, you might need to adjust the resistor value or check for faulty components.

6. **Check the LED**:

o If the circuit seems to be connected properly but the LED doesn't light up, try replacing the LED with a new one. It's possible that the LED is damaged or defective.

Understanding Circuit Behavior

Once your circuit is functioning, it's important to understand why it behaves the way it does. Here's a quick overview of the key behaviors at play in this simple LED circuit:

1. **Current Flow**:
   - When the circuit is closed and the power is supplied, current flows from the positive terminal of the power source, through the resistor, through the LED, and then back to the ground.
   - The resistor limits the current to ensure the LED is not overloaded, and the LED emits light when current passes through it.

2. **Voltage Drop**:
   - Every component in the circuit (e.g., the LED and resistor) causes a **voltage drop**. The total voltage from the power supply is divided between the components based on their resistance.
   - For example, if you're using a 5V power supply, the resistor will drop some of the voltage, and the LED will drop a portion of the voltage based on its forward voltage rating (typically around 1.8V to 3.3V for different types of LEDs).

3. **Resistor's Role**:
   - The resistor ensures that the LED receives the right amount of current. If the resistor were too small, the current would be too high, possibly burning out the LED. If the resistor were too large, the LED would not receive enough current and wouldn't light up properly.

○ The value of the resistor can be calculated using **Ohm's Law**: R=Vtotal−VLEDILEDR = \frac{V_{\text{total}} - V_{\text{LED}}}{I_{\text{LED}}}R=ILED Vtotal−VLED Where:

- VtotalV_{\text{total}}Vtotal is the power supply voltage (5V in our example),
- VLEDV_{\text{LED}}VLED is the voltage drop across the LED (usually 2V for standard red LEDs),
- ILEDI_{\text{LED}}ILED is the desired current through the LED (typically around 20mA for standard LEDs).

In this case, the resistor would be approximately:

R=5V−2V0.02A=150 ΩR = \frac{5V - 2V}{0.02A} = 150\ \OmegaR=0.02A5V−2V=150 Ω

So a 220Ω resistor would be a good choice to ensure the LED isn't overloaded.

Conclusion

In this chapter, you've learned how to build a simple LED circuit, how to test and troubleshoot it, and how to understand its behavior. Working with basic circuits is the first step in understanding electronics and will prepare you for more complex projects. As you gain more experience, you'll start to see how circuits are designed to meet specific needs and how you can combine different components to create useful, functional systems. Whether you're creating a simple circuit or building something more advanced, these fundamental concepts will be the foundation for your future projects.

CHAPTER 16

UNDERSTANDING OSCILLATORS AND CLOCKS

What Are Oscillators?

An **oscillator** is an electronic circuit that produces a periodic, oscillating signal, typically a **sine wave**, **square wave**, or **triangle wave**. Oscillators are crucial in many electronic applications because they generate consistent timing signals used to drive various components and systems.

The primary function of an oscillator is to generate a regular, repetitive signal without requiring an external signal to maintain the oscillation. This signal can then be used for timing, frequency generation, or synchronization in a wide range of electronic systems.

Oscillators are often found in applications where precise timing or periodicity is required, such as **clocks**, **radio transmitters**, **signal generators**, and **audio systems**.

Types of Oscillators:

- **Sinusoidal Oscillators**: Generate smooth, continuous sine waves. They are often used in radio-frequency applications or signal processing.
- **Square Wave Oscillators**: Produce a square wave, alternating between high and low states. They are commonly used in digital circuits, clocks, and timers.
- **Relaxation Oscillators**: Use the charging and discharging of capacitors or inductors to generate periodic pulses. These are commonly used in timing applications and signal generation.

Their Role in Creating Periodic Signals

Oscillators play a vital role in creating periodic signals, which are fundamental for synchronization and timing in electronic circuits. These periodic signals can be used for various purposes:

1. **Clock Generation**:
   o Oscillators are used in **clock circuits** to provide a stable timing signal for digital systems, including microcontrollers, processors, and memory.
   o For example, a microcontroller may rely on an external clock oscillator to synchronize its operations, ensuring that instructions are executed at the correct speed.
2. **Frequency Generation**:

- o Oscillators generate precise frequencies, which are used in communication systems (like radios), test equipment (such as frequency generators), and audio systems (like synthesizers).
- o For instance, a radio transmitter might use an oscillator to generate a specific frequency, which is then modulated to carry information.

3. **Pulse Generation**:
- o Some oscillators generate periodic pulses, which can be used to trigger other circuits. For example, a pulse generator can be used to control the timing of events in digital circuits, such as shifting data between registers or activating motors in robotics.

4. **Timing and Synchronization**:
- o Oscillators ensure that different parts of a system operate in sync. For example, they synchronize the clock signals in computers or control the timing of events in digital communication systems.

Example: Using a 555 Timer to Generate Clock Signals

The **555 timer** IC is one of the most commonly used oscillators in electronics. It can be configured in different modes, but one of the most popular uses is to generate periodic clock signals, often in the form of a square wave. This is particularly useful for timing applications, such as creating a clock pulse or generating a delay.

Components Needed:

- 555 Timer IC
- 220Ω resistor
- 10kΩ resistor
- 100nF capacitor
- LED (optional)
- Breadboard and jumper wires
- Power supply (e.g., 5V or 9V battery)

Steps to Set Up the 555 Timer as an Oscillator:

1. **Understanding the 555 Timer Configuration**: The 555 timer IC can be set up in different modes:
   - **Astable Mode**: This is the most common mode for generating clock pulses. In astable mode, the 555 timer continually switches between its high and low states, generating a square wave.
   - **Monostable Mode**: In this mode, the 555 timer produces a single pulse in response to an external trigger.

For generating periodic signals, we'll use the **astable mode**.

2. **Wiring the 555 Timer**:
   o Connect the **VCC** pin (pin 8) of the 555 timer to the positive voltage supply (5V or 9V).
   o Connect the **GND** pin (pin 1) to the ground.
   o Connect the **Trigger** (pin 2) to **Threshold** (pin 6). These two pins work together to set the timing cycle.
   o Place a **220Ω resistor** between **pin 7** (Discharge) and **pin 6** (Threshold).
   o Place a **10kΩ resistor** between **pin 6** (Threshold) and **pin 8** (VCC).
   o Connect a **100nF capacitor** between **pin 6** (Threshold) and **pin 1** (GND).
   o Optionally, connect an **LED** with a current-limiting resistor between pin 3 (Output) and GND to visualize the clock signal.

3. **Understanding the Timing Calculation**: The output frequency (the rate at which the 555 timer switches between high and low states) can be calculated using the following formula:

$$f = \frac{1.44}{(R1 + 2 \times R2) \times C}$$

Where:

- **R1** is the resistor between VCC and pin 7 (Discharge).
- **R2** is the resistor between pins 7 and 6 (Threshold).
- **C** is the capacitor between pins 6 and 1 (Ground).
- **f** is the frequency of the clock output.

For our circuit:

- R1 = 220Ω
- R2 = 10kΩ
- C = 100nF

Substituting these values into the formula will give us the frequency at which the 555 timer generates the clock pulse.

4. **Testing the Circuit**:
   - Once everything is connected, power up the circuit. The LED should blink on and off, indicating that the 555 timer is generating a clock signal.
   - You can adjust the frequency by changing the values of R1, R2, or the capacitor C to modify the timing cycle (blink rate).

5. **Observe the Output on an Oscilloscope (Optional)**: If you have access to an oscilloscope, you can connect it to pin 3 (the output pin) to view the waveform generated by the 555 timer. You should see a square wave, with a defined high and low state.

Why Use the 555 Timer?

The **555 timer** is widely used for generating clock signals because it is inexpensive, versatile, and easy to use. It can be configured for different types of timing tasks, such as creating precise delays, pulse-width modulation (PWM), and generating clock pulses for various systems, such as microcontrollers or frequency generators.

Conclusion

In this chapter, you've learned about **oscillators** and their essential role in electronics, generating periodic signals that drive timing, synchronization, and signal processing in systems. We discussed the use of the **555 timer** as an oscillator to generate clock signals, a common task in embedded systems and digital circuits. Understanding oscillators and how to configure and use them in projects like clock generation is fundamental for building more complex systems, whether in robotics, communication devices, or consumer electronics.

CHAPTER 17

INTRODUCTION TO ANALOG AND DIGITAL SIGNALS

What's the Difference Between Analog and Digital Signals?

In electronics, signals are used to represent information. These signals can take different forms, primarily **analog** and **digital**. Both have their uses in various applications, and understanding their differences is essential when working with electronic systems.

1. **Analog Signals**:
    - **Definition**: An analog signal is a continuous signal that varies over time and can take any value within a given range. These signals represent real-world phenomena that change smoothly and continuously, such as temperature, sound, or light intensity.
    - **Characteristics**:
        - **Continuous**: Analog signals are continuous, meaning they can have an

140

infinite number of values within their range.

- **Representation**: Analog signals are often represented by a smooth, flowing wave, like a sine wave or a ramp wave.

- **Example**: The voltage produced by a microphone as it captures sound is an analog signal. The sound pressure (loudness) changes continuously in real-time.

2. **Digital Signals**:

  o **Definition**: A digital signal is a discrete signal that represents information using binary values: **0** (low) and **1** (high). Digital signals are step-based and switch between these two states.

  o **Characteristics**:

    - **Discrete**: Unlike analog signals, digital signals can only have specific values, usually 0 or 1, and change at distinct intervals.

    - **Representation**: Digital signals are often depicted as square waves with abrupt transitions between high and low states.

    - **Example**: A computer processor uses digital signals to carry out operations. Each bit of data is either 0 or 1, representing information in a binary format.

Key Differences:

- **Smooth vs. Step**: Analog signals are smooth and continuous, while digital signals change abruptly between discrete states (0 or 1).
- **Precision**: Analog signals can represent infinite values, while digital signals can only represent a limited number of values (though more can be achieved through encoding techniques).
- **Noise Resistance**: Digital signals are more resistant to noise and degradation over long distances compared to analog signals, which can lose quality due to interference.

Real-World Examples: Audio vs. Digital Signals

To better understand the difference between analog and digital signals, let's look at two real-world examples: **audio signals** and **digital signals** in computers.

1. **Audio Signals (Analog)**:
   o **Analog Audio**: Audio signals are traditionally analog in nature. When you speak into a microphone or play an instrument, the sound

waves are continuous, meaning they vary smoothly in amplitude and frequency.

- o **Example**: An **analog audio signal** is created when sound waves travel through the air and are captured by a microphone. The microphone converts the air pressure variations (sound) into a continuous electrical signal, which is sent to amplifiers or audio processing systems.

- o **Challenges**: Analog audio signals are susceptible to noise and distortion, especially over long distances or when amplified. This is why analog recordings, such as vinyl records or cassette tapes, can degrade in quality over time.

2. **Digital Audio**:

- o **Digital Audio**: Digital audio, on the other hand, represents sound using discrete values. This is done by converting an analog audio signal into a series of binary numbers (digital signals) through a process called **sampling**.

- o **Example**: **CD audio** is an example of digital audio. The sound from a microphone is sampled at specific intervals (typically 44,100 times per second for standard audio CDs) and quantized into discrete values, which are then encoded into binary form.

o **Advantages**: Digital audio can be stored, processed, and transmitted with minimal degradation in quality. Even if there is some interference, the digital signal can be reconstructed, ensuring that the audio quality remains high.

How to Convert Between Analog and Digital Signals

Converting between analog and digital signals is essential in modern electronics, where devices often need to interact with both types of signals. There are two primary processes involved in these conversions: **Analog-to-Digital Conversion (ADC)** and **Digital-to-Analog Conversion (DAC)**.

1. **Analog-to-Digital Conversion (ADC)**:
   o **Definition**: ADC is the process of converting a continuous analog signal into a discrete digital signal. This is essential for microcontrollers, computers, and digital audio systems, which can only process digital data.
   o **How It Works**:
     ▪ **Sampling**: The analog signal is sampled at regular intervals to capture the signal's value at those points in time. The rate at

144

which samples are taken is known as the **sampling rate** (e.g., 44.1kHz in audio).

- **Quantization**: The sampled values are then rounded off to the nearest discrete value based on the resolution of the ADC. This step is known as **quantization** and introduces a small error called **quantization noise**.

- **Encoding**: The quantized values are then encoded into a digital format (binary numbers) that can be processed by digital systems.

o **Example**: A **sound card** in a computer uses an ADC to convert the analog audio signal from a microphone into a digital signal that can be processed, stored, or transmitted.

2. **Digital-to-Analog Conversion (DAC)**:

   o **Definition**: DAC is the process of converting a discrete digital signal back into a continuous analog signal. This is used when digital systems need to drive analog devices, such as speakers, or when creating analog waveforms for various applications.

   o **How It Works**:

     - **Reconstruction**: A DAC reconstructs the original analog signal by taking the discrete digital values and converting them into a continuous waveform. The DAC does this by applying a series of steps to approximate the original analog signal.

- **Filtering**: The output of a DAC may have high-frequency noise or jagged steps. This noise is typically smoothed out using a **low-pass filter**, resulting in a smooth analog output.

o **Example**: A **digital music player** uses a DAC to convert the digital audio file (e.g., MP3) into an analog signal that can drive a speaker, allowing you to hear the sound.

Real-World Conversion Example: Audio in a Digital Recorder

- **Step 1 (ADC)**: When recording audio using a microphone connected to a digital recorder, the microphone captures the continuous analog sound waves. The ADC samples the sound waves at a specified rate (e.g., 44.1kHz) and converts each sample into a digital number.

- **Step 2 (Digital Storage)**: The digital audio file (such as a WAV or MP3 file) is then stored on the recorder or computer as a sequence of digital values (binary numbers).

- **Step 3 (DAC)**: When playing back the audio, a DAC in the recorder or computer converts the digital audio file back into an analog signal, which is then sent to a speaker, allowing you to hear the sound as it was originally recorded.

Conclusion

In this chapter, we've explored the key differences between analog and digital signals, their roles in electronics, and how to convert between them. Analog signals are continuous and smooth, representing real-world phenomena like sound and temperature, while digital signals are discrete and binary, offering precision and resistance to noise. The process of converting analog to digital and vice versa—via ADCs and DACs—is crucial for modern devices that need to interact with both types of signals. Whether it's for audio processing, sensor readings, or communication, understanding these concepts will help you design systems that efficiently handle both analog and digital data.

CHAPTER 18

UNDERSTANDING LOGIC GATES AND BOOLEAN ALGEBRA

What Are Logic Gates?

Logic gates are fundamental building blocks of digital electronics. A **logic gate** is an electronic component that takes one or more binary inputs (0s and 1s) and produces a single binary output (also 0 or 1) based on a specific logical function. These gates implement **Boolean functions**, which are the basis of digital circuits and systems. Logic gates perform simple operations like AND, OR, NOT, NAND, NOR, XOR, and XNOR, which form the foundation for more complex digital circuits.

Each logic gate performs a specific logical operation, which can be expressed as a **truth table**—a table that shows all possible input combinations and their corresponding outputs.

Here are the basic logic gates:

1. **AND Gate**:

- o **Operation**: The AND gate outputs 1 only if **both** inputs are 1. Otherwise, it outputs 0.
- o **Truth Table**:

Input A	Input B	Output (A AND B)
0	0	0
0	1	0
1	0	0
1	1	1

2. **OR Gate**:
- o **Operation**: The OR gate outputs 1 if **either** of the inputs is 1. If both are 0, the output is 0.
- o **Truth Table**:

Input A	Input B	Output (A OR B)
0	0	0
0	1	1
1	0	1
1	1	1

3. **NOT Gate (Inverter)**:
   - ○ **Operation**: The NOT gate inverts the input. If the input is 1, the output is 0, and vice versa.
   - ○ **Truth Table**:

Input	Output (NOT A)
0	1
1	0

4. **NAND Gate**:
   - ○ **Operation**: The NAND gate is the opposite of the AND gate. It outputs 0 only when both inputs are 1. For all other input combinations, it outputs 1.
   - ○ **Truth Table**:

Input A	Input B	Output (A NAND B)
0	0	1
0	1	1
1	0	1
1	1	0

5. **NOR Gate**:

- o **Operation**: The NOR gate is the opposite of the OR gate. It outputs 1 only when both inputs are 0. For all other combinations, it outputs 0.
- o **Truth Table**:

Input A	Input B	Output (A NOR B)
0	0	1
0	1	0
1	0	0
1	1	0

6. **XOR Gate (Exclusive OR)**:
- o **Operation**: The XOR gate outputs 1 if **only one** of the inputs is 1, but not both. It's often used for operations like parity checking.
- o **Truth Table**:

Input A	Input B	Output (A XOR B)
0	0	0
0	1	1

Input A	Input B	Output (A XOR B)
1	0	1
1	1	0

7. XNOR Gate (Exclusive NOR):

- o **Operation**: The XNOR gate is the opposite of the XOR gate. It outputs 1 when the inputs are equal (either both 0 or both 1).
- o **Truth Table**:

Input A	Input B	Output (A XNOR B)
0	0	1
0	1	0
1	0	0
1	1	1

The Role of Logic Gates in Digital Electronics

Logic gates play a pivotal role in **digital electronics**. They are the foundation of digital systems, allowing the creation of circuits that perform complex calculations, decision-making, and control tasks. Logic gates are used in a variety of applications:

1. **Combinational Logic Circuits**:
   - Logic gates are combined to create **combinational circuits**, where the output depends only on the current inputs. Examples include **adders** (for addition), **multiplexers** (for routing data), and **decoders** (for signal conversion).

2. **Sequential Logic Circuits**:
   - Sequential circuits use memory elements (like flip-flops) along with logic gates to create circuits that depend on both the current inputs and past states (i.e., they have a "memory"). These circuits are used to implement **counters**, **shift registers**, and **state machines**.

3. **Arithmetic and Logic Units (ALUs)**:
   - The **ALU**, which is the core of a microprocessor, uses logic gates to perform arithmetic (addition, subtraction, etc.) and logical (AND, OR, NOT, etc.) operations.

4. **Control Units**:
   - Logic gates help in creating the **control unit** of a computer, which manages the operation of the

processor by sending control signals to other parts of the computer.

5. **Data Storage and Memory**:
    o   Logic gates are used in memory devices, including **SRAM** (Static RAM) and **DRAM** (Dynamic RAM), where they control the storage and retrieval of data.

Real-World Example: How Logic Gates Are Used in Computers

Logic gates are the backbone of all digital electronics, and their applications in computers are extensive:

1. **Data Processing**:
    o   The **Arithmetic Logic Unit (ALU)** of a computer processor performs arithmetic and logical operations. For example, an **AND** gate might be used to compare two bits (e.g., checking if two binary numbers are equal), while an **OR** gate could be used to perform a logical addition in binary arithmetic.
2. **Memory Storage**:
    o   **Flip-flops**, which are made from combinations of logic gates, store individual bits of data. These flip-flops can be combined to form registers and

memory cells, which are used to hold data in computers.

- o For instance, a **D flip-flop**, created using NAND gates, is used in memory storage to store a bit of data (0 or 1) until it's needed.

3. **Control Units**:
   - o The **control unit** in a computer is responsible for fetching instructions, decoding them, and executing them in the correct sequence. Logic gates are used to create the circuits that manage this operation. For example, logic gates can decode an instruction and determine which part of the processor should execute it.

4. **Multiplexing and Demultiplexing**:
   - o In computers, **multiplexers (MUX)** and **demultiplexers (DEMUX)** are used to manage data flow. These devices rely on logic gates to route data to the appropriate location within the system. For example, a multiplexer might use logic gates to select one of several data lines based on a control signal.

5. **Error Detection and Correction**:
   - o Logic gates are also used in systems designed for **error detection and correction**, such as **parity bits** (which are based on XOR gates). These systems ensure that data sent between devices is

accurate and has not been corrupted during transmission.

Conclusion

In this chapter, we explored **logic gates**, the fundamental building blocks of digital electronics. These gates perform basic logical operations that form the core of **combinational** and **sequential circuits**. From **microprocessors** to **memory storage**, logic gates play a vital role in processing, controlling, and storing information in electronic systems. Understanding logic gates and how they combine to form complex digital systems is essential for anyone working with digital electronics or embedded systems. Whether you're designing simple circuits or building advanced microprocessor systems, logic gates are at the heart of your designs.

CHAPTER 19

THE WORLD OF PRINTED CIRCUIT BOARDS (PCBS)

What Are PCBs and Why Are They Essential?

A **Printed Circuit Board (PCB)** is a flat board used to physically support and electrically connect electronic components. It is a critical element in most modern electronic devices, providing the foundation on which the components are mounted and interconnected. PCBs are used in everything from small consumer electronics like smartphones to large-scale devices like computers, medical equipment, and industrial machines.

Why Are PCBs Essential?:

1. **Component Organization**: PCBs provide a structured layout for electronic components, such as resistors, capacitors, and microcontrollers, making it easier to assemble and maintain complex circuits.
2. **Electrical Connections**: PCBs use conductive copper traces to create electrical paths between components, allowing the transmission of signals and power.

3. **Reliability**: PCBs improve the reliability of a circuit by providing stable connections and minimizing the risk of short circuits, signal interference, or loose connections that can occur in breadboard or wire-wrapped circuits.

4. **Space Efficiency**: By compactly arranging components on a single board, PCBs reduce the need for bulky wiring, which saves space and allows for the miniaturization of devices.

5. **Cost-Effectiveness**: PCBs are easy to mass-produce, making them a cost-effective solution for assembling electronics on a large scale.

PCBs are found in virtually every modern electronic device, and they are fundamental to the operation and assembly of electronic circuits. Without PCBs, it would be difficult to build complex, reliable, and compact electronic systems.

How PCBs Are Designed and Manufactured

Designing and manufacturing a PCB involves multiple steps, from circuit design to fabricating the board and assembling components. Let's break down the process:

1. **Circuit Design**:

- o **Schematic Design**: The first step in designing a PCB is creating a schematic, which is a diagram showing how the components in the circuit are connected. This is typically done using **CAD (Computer-Aided Design)** software like **Eagle, KiCad**, or **Altium Designer**.
  - ▪ The schematic shows the components (e.g., resistors, capacitors, ICs) and their electrical connections. It serves as a blueprint for the PCB layout.
- o **Choosing Components**: The components need to be selected based on the electrical requirements of the circuit. Each component has a unique footprint that defines its physical size and pin layout on the PCB.
- o **Netlist Creation**: The schematic software generates a netlist, which is a list of electrical connections that will guide the placement of components on the PCB.

2. **PCB Layout**:
  - o **Component Placement**: After the schematic is complete, the next step is to arrange the components on the PCB. This step is crucial, as the components must be placed in such a way that minimizes trace lengths, reduces interference, and ensures proper heat dissipation.

- o **Routing**: The next step is routing the copper traces that connect the pins of components. These traces are the electrical pathways through which current flows, and they must be laid out to avoid short circuits or signal degradation.
- o **Layer Design**: PCBs can be single-layer (one layer of copper), double-layer, or multi-layer (with multiple copper layers sandwiched between insulating layers). More layers allow for more complex circuits but can increase cost.
- o **Design Rules Check (DRC)**: After the routing is complete, the design must be checked for any errors, such as traces that are too close together or components placed incorrectly. CAD software typically includes a DRC feature to identify and correct potential issues.

3. **Fabrication**:
- o **Printing the PCB**: Once the layout is finalized, the design files are sent to a PCB manufacturer. The manufacturer uses a process called **photolithography** to transfer the PCB design onto a copper-clad board.
  - ▪ **Step 1**: A thin layer of copper is applied to an insulating material (usually fiberglass).

- **Step 2**: A photoresist material is applied to the copper surface, and the PCB design is projected onto the material using ultraviolet light. This creates a pattern where copper will be kept and the rest will be etched away.

- **Step 3**: The PCB is exposed to a chemical etchant that removes the unwanted copper, leaving the desired copper traces on the board.

- **Step 4**: After etching, the PCB is cleaned and the holes for the components are drilled. For multi-layer PCBs, additional layers are bonded together.

4. **Testing**:

   o After fabrication, the PCB undergoes various testing procedures to ensure it is functioning as expected. This includes:

   - **Electrical Testing**: Checking for continuity, correct voltage levels, and correct signal routing.

   - **Visual Inspection**: Inspecting for physical defects such as misplaced components or poor solder joints.

- **Automated Optical Inspection (AOI)**: Using cameras and software to automatically detect defects on the PCB.

5. **Assembly**:

   o **Soldering Components**: Once the PCB is fabricated and tested, components are soldered onto the board. This can be done manually or using machines like **pick-and-place machines** that automate the placement and soldering process.

      - **Through-Hole Soldering**: For components with leads that go through the PCB, the leads are inserted, and the board is soldered on both sides.

      - **Surface-Mount Soldering**: For components without leads (SMD), the components are placed on the surface of the board, and soldering is done using reflow soldering techniques.

6. **Final Testing and Quality Control**:

   o After the PCB is fully assembled, the final product undergoes another round of testing to ensure everything works as expected. This includes functional testing, power-on testing, and stress testing.

162

Example: Designing a Simple PCB for Your Project

Let's walk through the steps of designing a simple PCB for a basic LED circuit, similar to the one we discussed earlier in Chapter 15.

1. Circuit Design (Schematic):

- **Components**:
    - LED
    - Resistor (220Ω to 330Ω)
    - Microcontroller (optional, if you want to control the LED with a microcontroller)
- **Connections**:
    - Connect the anode of the LED to the output pin of the microcontroller (or to a voltage source).
    - Connect the cathode of the LED to the ground via the resistor.

2. PCB Layout:

- In your CAD software (e.g., Eagle), start by placing the components on the PCB. Position the LED and resistor in such a way that the traces (the copper paths) connecting

163

them are as short as possible to reduce resistance and improve efficiency.

- Route the copper traces between the components, ensuring that the signal paths don't cross over each other to prevent short circuits.
- Once the layout is complete, run a design rule check to ensure that the trace widths are sufficient for the current that will flow through them and that there are no violations.

3. Fabrication:

- After completing the design, generate the **Gerber files** from the CAD software. These files are the standard format used by PCB manufacturers to fabricate the boards.
- Send these files to a PCB manufacturer to have the board made. For simple projects, many online services offer **quick-turn PCB fabrication** at affordable prices.

4. Assembly:

- Once the PCB is delivered, solder the components onto the board. For a simple LED circuit, you'll need to solder the LED and resistor to their respective pads, ensuring a secure connection.

- If you're using a microcontroller, you'll need to solder the microcontroller and possibly other components like capacitors or diodes for protection.

5. Testing:

- Once assembled, connect the PCB to a power source and test the circuit. The LED should light up when the power is applied. If there's an issue (e.g., the LED doesn't light up), you'll need to troubleshoot the connections, verify the component values, or test for any possible short circuits.

Conclusion

In this chapter, we've explored **Printed Circuit Boards (PCBs)**—what they are, why they're essential, and how they are designed and manufactured. PCBs provide a reliable, space-efficient, and cost-effective solution for connecting and organizing components in electronic devices. By understanding the process of designing, fabricating, and assembling PCBs, you can create your own electronic circuits and take on more complex projects. Whether you're building a simple LED circuit or a sophisticated microcontroller-based design, mastering the basics of PCBs is essential for success in electronics design and development.

CHAPTER 20

INTRODUCTION TO ROBOTICS AND ELECTRONICS

How Electronics and Robotics Intersect

Robotics is the field of engineering and technology that involves the design, construction, operation, and use of robots. Electronics is a crucial part of robotics because it forms the backbone of the robot's functions, from its sensors and actuators to its control systems and communication systems.

Here's how electronics and robotics intersect:

1. **Sensors**:
   - Sensors are electronic components that allow robots to perceive their environment. These sensors can detect a wide range of physical properties, such as distance, temperature, motion, and light. Examples of sensors in robotics include **infrared sensors** for distance measurement, **accelerometers** for motion detection, and **cameras** for vision.

o   The data from these sensors is processed by the robot's control system (often a microcontroller or microprocessor) to make decisions and enable interaction with the environment.

2. **Actuators**:

o   Actuators are the components that allow robots to perform physical tasks. These are often **motors** (e.g., DC motors, servos, or stepper motors) that move parts of the robot, such as wheels, arms, or robotic grippers.

o   Motors and other actuators are driven by electronic circuits controlled by the robot's microcontroller or other processing units.

3. **Control Systems**:

o   The control system is the "brain" of the robot. It processes data from sensors and sends commands to actuators to perform tasks. The control system is typically based on a **microcontroller** (e.g., Arduino, Raspberry Pi, or ESP32) that runs a program or algorithm to control the robot's behavior.

o   This system uses **logic circuits**, **timing signals**, and communication protocols (like I2C, SPI, or UART) to coordinate the actions of the robot.

4. **Power Supply**:

o Robots rely on an efficient power supply system to provide power to the sensors, actuators, and control systems. Most robots use rechargeable **batteries**, such as **Li-ion** or **Li-Po** batteries, which are lightweight and provide sufficient power for long operation times.

5. **Communication Systems**:

o Many robots also require **communication** to interact with other robots, remote controllers, or even the internet. Communication can be done through **wired** (e.g., USB or serial ports) or **wireless** systems (e.g., Bluetooth, Wi-Fi, Zigbee).

o These systems allow robots to receive commands, transmit data, or interact with other devices in a network.

By combining these electronic components and systems, robots can perform complex tasks autonomously or be controlled remotely.

Basic Components of a Robot

A robot typically consists of the following basic components:

1. **Power Supply**:
   - o The robot's power supply, usually a battery, provides the energy needed to run the various parts of the robot. Depending on the robot's size and purpose, this could be a small rechargeable battery or a larger power pack.

2. **Microcontroller**:
   - o The **microcontroller** or **microprocessor** serves as the robot's brain. It processes inputs from the sensors, performs computations, and sends control signals to the actuators. Popular microcontrollers for beginners include the **Arduino**, **Raspberry Pi**, and **ESP32**.

3. **Sensors**:
   - o Sensors allow robots to interact with their environment. They provide feedback to the microcontroller to help the robot understand its surroundings.
     - **Ultrasonic Sensors**: Used for distance measurement (e.g., obstacle avoidance).
     - **Infrared Sensors**: Used for proximity detection or line-following.
     - **Cameras**: Used for vision and object recognition.
     - **Gyroscopes/Accelerometers**: Used for orientation and movement detection.

4. **Actuators (Motors)**:

   o   Actuators enable robots to move and perform tasks. The most common actuators in robots are motors, which can be used for movement or control of limbs and other parts.

   - **DC Motors**: Often used in mobile robots for movement.
   - **Servo Motors**: Used for precise control of angles (e.g., robotic arms).
   - **Step Motors**: Provide precise movement and positioning.

5. **Chassis**:

   o   The chassis is the physical structure that holds all of the robot's components in place. It can be made from various materials, such as plastic, metal, or composite materials, and it provides support for the motors, sensors, and microcontroller.

6. **Communication Systems**:

   o   Many robots have the ability to communicate with external devices or other robots. Communication can be wired (e.g., USB) or wireless (e.g., Bluetooth, Wi-Fi, Zigbee).

   o   **Wireless Communication** is often used in autonomous robots or robots that are controlled remotely by a user.

7. **Software**:

   ○ The software, often called **firmware**, runs on the robot's microcontroller. It includes the algorithms and logic that allow the robot to make decisions, process sensor data, and control actuators.

   ○ **Programming languages** such as C, C++, Python, or specialized software like **Scratch** (for beginners) or **ROS** (Robot Operating System) can be used to develop software for robots.

Hands-On Project: Building a Simple Robot

In this hands-on project, we will build a simple robot that can move forward and backward using **DC motors** and avoid obstacles with an **ultrasonic sensor**. This basic robot will demonstrate how the components work together to perform tasks.

Components Needed:

- **Arduino Uno** (or any similar microcontroller)
- **2 DC motors** with wheels
- **L298N motor driver** (to control motors)
- **Ultrasonic sensor** (HC-SR04) for distance measurement

- **Chassis** (you can use a pre-made chassis or create your own)
- **Jumper wires**
- **9V battery** (for powering the motors and Arduino)
- **Breadboard** (optional, for prototyping connections)
- **Motor wheels** (attached to the DC motors)

Steps:

1. **Assemble the Chassis**:
   - Mount the **DC motors** onto the chassis and attach the wheels. These will provide the robot with movement.

2. **Connect the Motor Driver**:
   - Connect the two DC motors to the **L298N motor driver**. The motor driver will control the motors based on the signals sent by the Arduino.
   - Connect the **motor driver's power** input to the **9V battery**, and connect the **ground** of the battery to the **Arduino**.
   - Connect the **IN1, IN2, IN3, and IN4** pins of the L298N motor driver to the **Arduino**'s digital pins.

3. **Connect the Ultrasonic Sensor**:
   - The **HC-SR04 ultrasonic sensor** has four pins: **VCC**, **Trig**, **Echo**, and **GND**.

- o Connect the **VCC** to the 5V pin on the Arduino and the **GND** to the ground.
- o Connect the **Trig** pin to a digital pin (e.g., pin 9 on the Arduino) and the **Echo** pin to another digital pin (e.g., pin 10 on the Arduino).

4. **Program the Arduino**:

- o Write a simple program to control the motors and use the ultrasonic sensor for obstacle avoidance.

Here's an example code for the basic robot:

cpp

```
#define trigPin 9
#define echoPin 10
#define motor1A 3
#define motor1B 4
#define motor2A 5
#define motor2B 6

void setup() {
  pinMode(trigPin, OUTPUT);
  pinMode(echoPin, INPUT);
  pinMode(motor1A, OUTPUT);
  pinMode(motor1B, OUTPUT);
  pinMode(motor2A, OUTPUT);
  pinMode(motor2B, OUTPUT);
  Serial.begin(9600);
}
```

```
void loop() {
  long duration, distance;

  digitalWrite(trigPin, LOW);
  delayMicroseconds(2);
  digitalWrite(trigPin, HIGH);
  delayMicroseconds(10);
  digitalWrite(trigPin, LOW);

  duration = pulseIn(echoPin, HIGH);
  distance = (duration / 2) / 29.1;

  Serial.print("Distance: ");
  Serial.println(distance);

  if (distance < 10) {
    stopRobot();
  } else {
    moveForward();
  }
  delay(100);
}

void moveForward() {
  digitalWrite(motor1A, HIGH);
  digitalWrite(motor1B, LOW);
  digitalWrite(motor2A, HIGH);
  digitalWrite(motor2B, LOW);
```

175

```
}

void stopRobot() {
  digitalWrite(motor1A, LOW);
  digitalWrite(motor1B, LOW);
  digitalWrite(motor2A, LOW);
  digitalWrite(motor2B, LOW);
}
```

5. **Test the Robot**:
   o Once the circuit is built and the code is uploaded, the robot should move forward until it detects an obstacle within 10 cm, at which point it will stop.

Troubleshooting Tips:

- Ensure that the motor driver is connected correctly to the motors and the Arduino.
- Make sure the ultrasonic sensor is aligned and properly connected to avoid incorrect distance measurements.
- If the robot does not move or the motors don't respond, check the wiring and make sure the motor driver is properly powered.

Conclusion

In this chapter, we introduced the world of **robotics** and its intersection with **electronics**. We learned how electronics components like **sensors, actuators,** and **microcontrollers** come together to create robots that can interact with their environment. Through a simple hands-on project, you now have a basic robot that can move and avoid obstacles. This is just the beginning—by experimenting with more sensors, actuators, and algorithms, you can create more complex robots with a variety of behaviors and functions.

CHAPTER 21

WORKING WITH DISPLAYS

Types of Displays: LED, LCD, OLED

Displays are essential components in many electronic projects, providing a visual output of data or status information. There are several types of displays commonly used in electronics, each with different advantages and use cases. Let's look at the three most common types of displays: **LED**, **LCD**, and **OLED**.

1. **LED (Light Emitting Diode)**:
    o   **Overview**: An LED is a semiconductor device that emits light when current flows through it. It is widely used as a basic display element in electronics.
    o   **Characteristics**:
        ▪   **Simple and Cost-Effective**: LEDs are inexpensive and straightforward to use for basic displays.
        ▪   **Variety of Uses**: LEDs can be used in a **seven-segment display** (for showing numbers or a few characters) or **multi-color displays** (using RGB LEDs).

178

- **Low Power**: LEDs consume very little power, making them ideal for battery-powered applications.
- **Common Applications**: Digital clocks, simple status indicators, and counters.

o **Example**: A seven-segment LED display used to show a number or character.

2. **LCD (Liquid Crystal Display)**:

  o **Overview**: LCDs are flat-panel displays that use liquid crystals to modulate light. They are commonly used in devices like digital watches, calculators, and smartphones.

  o **Characteristics**:

  - **Energy Efficient**: LCDs use much less power than traditional light-emitting displays, especially when displaying static information.
  - **Good for Text and Simple Graphics**: They are excellent for displaying text and simple graphics, though they are generally not as bright or vibrant as OLED displays.
  - **Backlit or Reflective**: Some LCDs are **backlit**, meaning they have a light source behind the screen, while others are

reflective, using ambient light for visibility.

- o **Common Applications**: Digital clocks, calculators, weather stations, and handheld devices.
- o **Example**: A 16x2 LCD display commonly used to show text in embedded systems.

3. **OLED (Organic Light Emitting Diode)**:
   - o **Overview**: OLED displays are made of organic materials that emit light when electricity is applied. They offer superior color quality and contrast compared to LCDs.
   - o **Characteristics**:
     - **Better Image Quality**: OLEDs produce bright, vivid colors and true blacks because each pixel emits its own light, unlike LCDs that rely on a backlight.
     - **Slim and Flexible**: OLED displays are thinner, lighter, and can be made flexible, making them ideal for compact and curved devices.
     - **Power Efficient for Dark Screens**: OLEDs consume less power when displaying dark images because black pixels are turned off.

- o **Common Applications**: High-end smartphones, wearables, televisions, and smartwatches.
- o **Example**: A small 128x128 OLED display used in portable projects and gadgets.

How to Interface Displays with Microcontrollers

Interfacing displays with microcontrollers allows you to display information such as text, numbers, or graphics. The process of interfacing depends on the type of display being used. Let's look at how to connect and use each type of display with microcontrollers.

1. **LED Display**:
   - o **Seven-Segment LED Display**:
     - A **seven-segment display** has seven LEDs arranged in a figure-eight shape. It is typically used to display numerical digits. Each segment can be turned on or off to form different digits.
     - **Interfacing**: Seven-segment displays are usually controlled by digital pins on the microcontroller. You can either connect each segment to a pin or use an external **driver IC** (like the **74HC595 shift**

register) to reduce the number of microcontroller pins required.

- **Code**: To display a number, you send the appropriate high/low signals to the segments.

2. **LCD Display**:
   o **16x2 LCD Display**:
      - The **16x2 LCD** display has 16 columns and 2 rows, allowing you to display up to 32 characters.
      - **Interfacing**: LCDs typically use a **parallel interface** with multiple data pins (usually 6 or 8) connected to the microcontroller. Alternatively, many LCDs use a **I2C adapter**, which reduces the number of connections to just two data lines (SDA and SCL).
      - **Code**: Libraries like **LiquidCrystal** (for parallel LCDs) or **Wire** (for I2C LCDs) are used to control the LCD. These libraries provide functions to initialize the display, set the cursor, and print text.

3. **OLED Display**:
   o **128x128 OLED Display**:
      - OLED displays are often smaller, with a resolution of 128x128 pixels or 128x64

pixels. They can display text, simple graphics, and images.

- **Interfacing**: OLED displays typically use an **I2C or SPI interface**, which requires fewer wires than parallel displays.
- **Code**: The **Adafruit_SSD1306** library (for I2C OLEDs) or similar libraries are used to initialize the OLED, draw text, or graphics. The library allows you to set the pixel colors, display images, and manipulate text on the screen.

Example Project: Creating a Digital Clock

Now let's create a simple digital clock using an **Arduino** microcontroller and a **16x2 LCD** display. The clock will show the current time, and we will simulate the time using the Arduino's built-in **millis()** function for simplicity. We'll also explore how to interface an **RTC module (Real-Time Clock)** for accurate timekeeping.

Components Needed:

- **Arduino Uno** (or any Arduino-compatible board)

- **16x2 LCD** display
- **RTC Module** (e.g., DS3231)
- **Jumper wires**
- **Breadboard**

Steps:

1. **Connect the LCD to the Arduino**:
   - For the **16x2 LCD**, if you are using an I2C adapter, you only need four connections:
     - **VCC** to 5V on Arduino
     - **GND** to ground on Arduino
     - **SDA** to A4 (on most Arduino boards)
     - **SCL** to A5 (on most Arduino boards)
2. **Connect the RTC Module**:
   - The **DS3231 RTC module** uses I2C communication, so connect the following:
     - **VCC** to 5V on Arduino
     - **GND** to ground on Arduino
     - **SDA** to A4 (on most Arduino boards)
     - **SCL** to A5 (on most Arduino boards)
3. **Install Libraries**:
   - Install the **LiquidCrystal_I2C** library for controlling the LCD and the **RTClib** library for interfacing with the RTC module. These can be

installed through the Arduino IDE's **Library Manager**.

4. **Write the Code**:

cpp

```cpp
#include <Wire.h>
#include <LiquidCrystal_I2C.h>
#include <RTClib.h>

LiquidCrystal_I2C lcd(0x27, 16, 2);    // LCD
address, width, height
RTC_DS3231 rtc;   // Create RTC object

void setup() {
  lcd.begin();
  lcd.backlight();  // Turn on the LCD backlight
  if (!rtc.begin()) {
    lcd.print("Couldn't find RTC");
    while (1);
  }
  rtc.adjust(DateTime(F(__DATE__),
F(__TIME__)));  // Set RTC to compile time
}

void loop() {
  DateTime now = rtc.now();

  // Display current time in HH:MM:SS format
```

185

```
lcd.setCursor(0, 0);
lcd.print("Time: ");
lcd.print(now.hour(), DEC);
lcd.print(":");
if (now.minute() < 10) lcd.print("0");
lcd.print(now.minute(), DEC);
lcd.print(":");
if (now.second() < 10) lcd.print("0");
lcd.print(now.second(), DEC);

delay(1000);  // Update every second
}
```

5. **Upload and Test**:
   o Upload the code to the Arduino and power the circuit. You should see the current time displayed on the LCD. The time will update every second.

Conclusion

In this chapter, we explored different types of displays— **LED, LCD**, and **OLED**—and learned how to interface them with microcontrollers for various applications. We also worked on a hands-on project, creating a simple **digital clock** using an Arduino and a 16x2 LCD display. By understanding how to use displays in your projects, you can enhance your electronics projects by providing valuable visual feedback, whether it's showing numbers, text, or graphics. Display technology is essential for interactive projects, making it easier to convey information to users and improve the user experience.

CHAPTER 22

POWER MANAGEMENT IN ELECTRONICS

Understanding Voltage Regulators and Power Supplies

Power management is a critical aspect of electronic circuit design. It involves controlling the voltage and current supplied to components to ensure they receive the proper levels of power for optimal performance. Power supplies and voltage regulators are essential components in this process.

1. **Power Supplies**:
    - o A **power supply** is a source of electrical power for an electronic circuit. Power supplies come in two main forms: **AC-to-DC** and **DC-to-DC** converters.
        - ▪ **AC-to-DC Power Supply**: Converts alternating current (AC) from a wall outlet into direct current (DC), which is used to power most electronic circuits. This is the most common type of power supply used in devices like computers, radios, and televisions.

188

- **DC-to-DC Power Supply**: Converts one DC voltage level to another DC voltage level, which is commonly used in battery-powered devices to provide the appropriate voltage to components.

o **Types of Power Supplies**:

- **Linear Power Supply**: A linear power supply provides a constant output voltage by dissipating excess energy as heat. While reliable, linear supplies are less efficient because of the heat generated.

- **Switching Power Supply**: A more efficient power supply that uses switching techniques to convert power, offering higher efficiency and less heat generation compared to linear supplies.

2. **Voltage Regulators**:

o **Voltage regulators** are devices that maintain a constant output voltage regardless of changes in input voltage or load conditions. They are often used in circuits where a stable voltage is required to operate the components safely and efficiently.

- **Linear Regulators**: Linear voltage regulators, such as the **7805** or **LM317**, are simple and easy to use. They provide

189

a stable output by dissipating excess power as heat.

- **Switching Regulators (Buck/Boost)**: These regulators are more efficient than linear regulators. They convert excess voltage to power the load without generating as much heat. **Buck regulators** step down the voltage, while **Boost regulators** step up the voltage.

Choosing the Right Power Source for Your Circuit

When choosing the right power source for your circuit, several factors must be considered:

1. **Voltage Requirements**:
   - The first step is to determine the voltage required by your circuit or components. Different electronic components (e.g., microcontrollers, sensors, LEDs) have specific voltage requirements. For example, an **Arduino Uno** operates on 5V, while an **ESP32** operates on 3.3V.
   - If your power source doesn't match the voltage required by the components, you'll need a **voltage**

regulator to step down (buck) or step up (boost) the voltage to the correct level.

2. **Current Requirements**:

   o Determine how much current your circuit requires. For instance, a simple LED circuit may need only a few milliamps, whereas a motor or servo might require hundreds of milliamps or even amperes.

   o Ensure that your power supply can provide enough current for the entire circuit without overloading. The total current required can be calculated by summing the current demands of each component in your circuit.

3. **Power Supply Type**:

   o **Battery vs. Wall Adapter**: Battery-powered devices, such as portable projects, require a battery as the power source. Depending on the voltage and current requirements, you can choose between **Li-ion batteries** (for higher capacity and rechargeability) or **AA/AAA batteries** (for simple, lower-power applications).

   o **USB Power**: For portable devices like smartphones, microcontrollers, and small gadgets, USB power is often used. A **USB power bank** or a **wall adapter** can provide a stable 5V output.

o **AC-to-DC Adapter**: For larger systems that require a constant power source, an **AC-to-DC adapter** (often 12V or 5V) is suitable for powering devices directly from a wall outlet.

4. **Efficiency and Heat Considerations**:

o In systems with high current or voltage fluctuations, using a **switching regulator** is often preferred over linear regulators because it is more efficient and generates less heat.

o For low-power, low-heat applications, **linear regulators** can be a simpler and cheaper choice.

Real-World Example: Powering a Mobile Device

Let's consider how power management works in the real world, specifically how mobile devices like smartphones are powered. These devices rely on **battery-powered systems** with **voltage regulators** to ensure stable operation.

1. **Battery**:

o **Lithium-Ion (Li-ion) Batteries**: Mobile devices typically use **Li-ion or Li-Po** batteries, which provide high energy density in a compact form. A typical smartphone battery operates at 3.7V to

4.2V, but the voltage may vary as the battery charges and discharges.

- o **Power Storage**: The battery stores electrical energy, and its charge level is monitored by a **battery management system** (BMS) to prevent overcharging or deep discharge.

2. **Voltage Regulation**:

- o **Step-Down Voltage Regulators (Buck Converter)**: Mobile devices use **buck converters** to step down the battery voltage (typically 3.7V) to a stable 1.8V, 3.3V, or 5V to power the various internal components like the processor, memory, and sensors.

- o **Step-Up Voltage Regulators (Boost Converter)**: In some cases, mobile devices need to step up the voltage to power certain peripherals or components that require higher voltages, such as the backlight of an LCD screen or USB ports for charging other devices.

3. **Power Management ICs (PMICs)**:

- o Mobile devices integrate **Power Management ICs (PMICs)**, which are complex circuits that manage battery charging, regulate voltages, and distribute power to different parts of the device. These ICs ensure that each part of the device receives the correct voltage and current for safe and efficient operation.

4. **Charging the Battery**:
   - o **AC-to-DC Adapter**: When a mobile device is plugged into an outlet, it is powered by an **AC-to-DC adapter** (such as a USB charger). The adapter converts the 110V or 220V AC power from the wall outlet into a stable 5V DC voltage.
   - o **USB Charging**: The device typically charges through a USB cable, which provides a 5V output from a power source (e.g., a wall adapter, computer, or power bank). The **charging circuitry** in the device manages the charging process, ensuring the battery is charged safely and efficiently.

5. **Power Optimization**:
   - o Mobile devices use advanced techniques like **dynamic voltage scaling** and **sleep modes** to optimize power consumption and extend battery life. For example, the processor may lower its operating voltage and frequency when the device is idle, reducing power usage.

Conclusion

In this chapter, we explored **power management** in electronics, focusing on **voltage regulators** and **power supplies**, and discussed how to choose the right power source for your circuit based on voltage, current, and efficiency requirements. We also looked at a real-world example of how mobile devices manage power, including **batteries**, **voltage regulation**, and **charging systems**. Understanding power management is essential for designing efficient and reliable electronic systems, whether you're working on battery-powered projects or larger systems requiring stable AC-to-DC conversion.

CHAPTER 23
TROUBLESHOOTING AND
REPAIRING CIRCUITS

Common Issues in Circuits

Troubleshooting is an essential skill when working with electronics. Circuits can encounter a variety of issues, and it's important to identify and resolve these problems efficiently. Below are some of the most common issues you might face in electronic circuits:

1. **No Power or Voltage**:
    o   **Symptoms**: The circuit does not turn on, and there is no voltage at the input or output points.
    o   **Possible Causes**:
        ▪   Power supply failure (e.g., battery dead, adapter not working).
        ▪   Broken or disconnected wires.
        ▪   Faulty or missing components (e.g., blown fuse or damaged resistor).
        ▪   Faulty power switch or button.

2. **Short Circuits**:

- o **Symptoms**: The circuit powers on briefly but then shuts off, or it continuously draws excessive current.
- o **Possible Causes**:
    - Wires or traces that are incorrectly connected, causing a direct path between the positive and negative terminals.
    - Faulty components that internally short, such as capacitors or ICs.
    - Solder bridges or shorts on the PCB.

3. **Overheating**:
    - o **Symptoms**: Components or the entire circuit gets excessively hot.
    - o **Possible Causes**:
        - Overvoltage or too much current being supplied to the circuit.
        - Incorrect or missing resistors leading to excessive current.
        - Power supply providing a voltage higher than required.
        - Components not rated for the current being drawn.

4. **Signal Issues**:
    - o **Symptoms**: Incorrect or distorted output signals.
    - o **Possible Causes**:

- Incorrect component values (e.g., wrong resistor or capacitor).
- Interference or noise affecting sensitive circuits, especially in high-speed or RF circuits.
- Faulty connections or loose wires that result in fluctuating signals.

5. **Component Failure**:
   - **Symptoms**: A specific component (e.g., LED, transistor, or motor) doesn't function as expected.
   - **Possible Causes**:
     - Overloading or over-voltage damage to components.
     - Environmental factors, like heat or humidity, causing degradation.
     - Manufacturing defects in components.

6. **Erratic Behavior or Unstable Circuit**:
   - **Symptoms**: Circuit works intermittently or behaves unpredictably.
   - **Possible Causes**:
     - Loose connections or poor solder joints causing intermittent contact.
     - Incorrect grounding or floating pins on ICs.
     - Faulty or weak power supply that fluctuates with load.

Tools and Techniques for Troubleshooting

To effectively troubleshoot a circuit, you'll need the right tools and techniques. Here are some of the most commonly used tools:

1. **Multimeter**:
   - o **Usage**: A multimeter is essential for measuring voltage, current, and resistance. It helps to identify issues like power supply failures, incorrect voltages, or short circuits.
     - **Voltage Measurement**: Set the multimeter to measure voltage (DC or AC depending on your circuit) and check the voltage at different points in the circuit.
     - **Continuity Test**: Use the continuity feature to check for broken or disconnected wires or solder joints.
     - **Resistance Measurement**: Measure the resistance across components to ensure they are functioning correctly (e.g., checking resistors, capacitors, or fuses).
2. **Oscilloscope**:

- o **Usage**: An oscilloscope is used to view and measure signal waveforms in circuits. It is especially useful for troubleshooting high-speed digital or analog circuits, as it allows you to visualize signal timing, shape, and noise.

  - **Waveform Analysis**: You can use an oscilloscope to inspect signals from sensors, microcontrollers, or other components that output time-dependent signals (e.g., clock signals or audio signals).

  - **Noise Detection**: An oscilloscope can help detect unwanted noise or voltage spikes in a signal that might indicate a problem.

3. **Power Supply with Adjustable Output**:

  - o **Usage**: An adjustable power supply allows you to control the voltage and current supplied to a circuit. This is especially useful when you need to test a circuit under different power conditions and troubleshoot power-related issues.

    - **Current Limiting**: Some power supplies allow you to limit the maximum current, preventing damage to the circuit during testing.

4. **Soldering Iron and Soldering Tools**:

o **Usage**: A good soldering iron is essential for repairing loose or broken connections. You may also need a desoldering pump or desoldering braid to remove excess solder and correct faulty solder joints.

- **Soldering**: Use the soldering iron to reflow solder on loose components or pins.
- **Desoldering**: If there is a short or a faulty component, you may need to desolder the component to replace it.

5. **Heat Gun**:

o **Usage**: A heat gun can be used to reflow solder on a surface-mount component (SMD) or to fix broken connections in delicate circuits.

6. **Visual Inspection**:

o **Usage**: Often, the cause of the issue can be spotted with a simple visual inspection. Look for burnt components, damaged traces, or misplaced parts. Inspect solder joints for cracks or cold solder joints, which can cause intermittent problems.

- **Inspect Components**: Check for any signs of damage or overheating, such as discoloration or burnt marks.

- **Check Soldering**: Make sure that there are no **cold joints** (solder joints that have not flowed correctly) or **solder bridges** (where solder connects two adjacent pins unintentionally).

Example: Repairing a Broken Circuit in a Household Device

Let's consider a scenario where a **household appliance** (e.g., a toaster, blender, or microwave) is not working properly. We'll go through the steps of troubleshooting and repairing a simple circuit.

Scenario: The toaster is not heating, and the indicator light does not come on.

Steps:

1. **Check the Power Supply**:
   o Use a multimeter to check if power is reaching the toaster. Set the multimeter to measure AC voltage (since the power supply is likely AC). Check the voltage at the power input of the toaster.

- o If no voltage is present, the issue may lie in the power cable or the fuse in the power supply. Check if the fuse is blown (use the continuity feature on the multimeter).

2. **Inspect the Switch and Controls**:

- o Check the toaster's power switch. Use the multimeter to check continuity across the switch when it is pressed. If no continuity is detected when the switch is pressed, it may be faulty and need replacement.
- o If there is continuity, move to the next stage to check the circuit path.

3. **Check the Heating Element**:

- o The heating element is likely the reason the toaster isn't heating. Use the multimeter to measure the resistance across the heating element. If the resistance is too high (infinity), the element is broken and needs to be replaced.
- o If the resistance is low (close to 0 ohms), the element is functional, and the issue may lie elsewhere.

4. **Inspect the Circuit Board**:

- o Open the toaster and visually inspect the circuit board for damaged components, burnt areas, or disconnected traces. Look for any **blown capacitors**, **burnt resistors**, or **damaged diodes**.

o If any components appear damaged, replace them. Use the soldering iron to remove the damaged component and solder in the new part.

5. **Test the Repair**:

o After replacing the damaged components, reassemble the toaster and test it again by plugging it in and pressing the switch. Use the multimeter to check the voltage across the heating element to ensure it is receiving power.

6. **Final Testing**:

o After confirming that the circuit is functioning properly, check the overall operation of the toaster. Test it several times to ensure that the issue has been resolved and that no further malfunctions occur.

Conclusion

In this chapter, we explored **common issues** in circuits, troubleshooting tools, and techniques. From identifying power issues to inspecting components and connections, effective troubleshooting relies on a combination of tools like the multimeter, oscilloscope, and soldering iron. We also went through an example of **repairing a broken circuit** in a household device, demonstrating a step-by-step approach to identifying and fixing issues. Troubleshooting is a crucial skill that will help you solve problems and maintain the reliability of your electronics projects and devices. By following a systematic approach, you can confidently diagnose and repair circuits, ensuring they work properly.

CHAPTER 24

ADVANCED MICROCONTROLLER PROJECTS

Building More Complex Projects with Microcontrollers

Microcontrollers (MCUs) are incredibly versatile and can be used for a wide range of applications, from simple LED blinkers to complex systems involving sensors, motors, and displays. As you gain experience with microcontrollers, you'll want to tackle more complex projects that require advanced techniques in circuit design, software programming, and system integration.

When building complex projects, there are a few important aspects to consider:

- **System Design**: Complex projects often involve more components, including sensors, actuators, and displays. You'll need to carefully design the system, considering how all the components will interact with each other and with the microcontroller.
- **Multiple I/O Operations**: More complex systems will require handling multiple inputs and outputs (I/O). This

can be achieved by using digital I/O, analog inputs, communication protocols (e.g., I2C, SPI), and timers.

- **Real-Time Operation**: As systems grow in complexity, real-time operations become important. Microcontrollers can handle real-time events like motor control, data logging, or sensor readings in real-time, but careful planning and efficient programming are required.

- **Power Management**: Many complex projects, especially those involving battery-powered devices, require careful power management to maximize battery life and ensure reliable operation.

Example: Controlling Multiple Devices with a Single Microcontroller

Let's explore an example where you control multiple devices with a single microcontroller, such as an **Arduino**. We'll design a system that controls a **servo motor**, reads data from a **temperature sensor**, and displays the data on an **LCD screen**.

Components Needed:

- **Arduino Uno** (or similar microcontroller)
- **Servo motor**

- **DHT11 or DHT22 temperature and humidity sensor**
- **16x2 LCD display (with I2C interface)**
- **Power supply** (e.g., 5V adapter or battery pack)
- **Jumper wires**
- **Breadboard**

System Overview:

- The **servo motor** will be controlled based on the temperature readings.
- The **DHT11/DHT22 sensor** will provide temperature and humidity data to the microcontroller.
- The **16x2 LCD display** will show the current temperature and humidity in real time.

Steps:

1. **Connect the Components**:
   - Connect the **servo motor** to one of the PWM pins on the Arduino (e.g., Pin 9).
   - Connect the **DHT11/DHT22 sensor** to a digital input pin (e.g., Pin 2). The sensor has three pins: VCC, GND, and DATA.
   - Connect the **16x2 LCD** to the Arduino's **SDA** and **SCL** pins for I2C communication (Pins A4 and A5 on an Arduino Uno).

2. **Write the Code**: The code will read the temperature from the DHT sensor, control the servo based on the temperature, and display the data on the LCD.

cpp

```cpp
#include <DHT.h>
#include <Wire.h>
#include <LiquidCrystal_I2C.h>
#include <Servo.h>

#define DHTPIN 2          // Pin connected to the
DHT sensor
#define DHTTYPE DHT11     // DHT 11 sensor
DHT dht(DHTPIN, DHTTYPE);  // Initialize DHT
sensor

LiquidCrystal_I2C lcd(0x27, 16, 2);   // I2C
address of LCD (0x27 for most models)
Servo myServo;  // Create a servo object

void setup() {
  lcd.begin(16, 2);   // Initialize the LCD
  lcd.backlight();    // Turn on the backlight
  dht.begin();        // Initialize the DHT sensor
  myServo.attach(9); // Connect servo to pin 9
}

void loop() {
```

```
// Read temperature and humidity
float h = dht.readHumidity();
float t = dht.readTemperature();  // Celsius

// Check if reading failed
if (isnan(h) || isnan(t)) {
  lcd.print("Failed to read from DHT sensor");
  return;
}

// Display temperature and humidity on LCD
lcd.clear();
lcd.setCursor(0, 0);
lcd.print("Temp: ");
lcd.print(t);
lcd.print(" C");
lcd.setCursor(0, 1);
lcd.print("Humidity: ");
lcd.print(h);
lcd.print(" %");

// Control servo based on temperature
if (t < 25) {
  myServo.write(0);  // Move servo to position
0 degrees if temperature is below 25
} else if (t >= 25 && t < 30) {
  myServo.write(90);   // Move servo to 90
degrees if temperature is between 25 and 30
} else {
```

```
myServo.write(180);    // Move servo to 180
degrees if temperature is above 30
  }


  delay(2000);    // Wait for 2 seconds before
taking the next reading
}
```

Code Explanation:

- **Libraries**: The `DHT` library is used to interact with the temperature and humidity sensor. The `Servo` library controls the servo motor, and the `LiquidCrystal_I2C` library manages the LCD display.
- **Reading Sensor Data**: The `dht.readTemperature()` function fetches the temperature from the sensor, and the `dht.readHumidity()` function reads the humidity.
- **Controlling the Servo**: Based on the temperature, the servo motor moves to a specific angle. If the temperature is below 25°C, the servo moves to 0°, between 25°C and 30°C, it moves to 90°, and above 30°C, it moves to 180°.
- **LCD Display**: The LCD displays the temperature and humidity readings in real time.

3. **Testing**:
   o Upload the code to the Arduino and power up the system. The LCD should display the current temperature and humidity, while the servo motor

should adjust its position based on the temperature readings.

How to Optimize Your Code for Performance

As your projects become more complex, optimizing your code for performance becomes increasingly important, especially when dealing with microcontrollers that have limited processing power and memory. Here are a few tips for optimizing your microcontroller code:

1. **Minimize Delays**:
   - **Use Non-Blocking Code**: Avoid using long `delay()` functions, as they halt the entire program. Instead, use **millis()** to create non-blocking delays. This allows the microcontroller to perform other tasks while waiting.
   - **Example**: Instead of `delay(1000);`, use `if (millis() - previousMillis >= interval) { // Do something }`.
2. **Efficient Memory Usage**:
   - **Use Appropriate Data Types**: Use the smallest data type that can hold your values (e.g., use `byte` or `uint8_t` for small numbers instead of `int` or `float`).

- o **Optimize Arrays**: If you are using large arrays, make sure they are necessary and minimize their size.
- o **Freeing Up Memory**: For large programs, try to free up memory by removing unnecessary variables or libraries when not in use.

3. **Interrupts**:

- o **Use Interrupts**: Interrupts are a powerful feature of microcontrollers that allow the processor to react to events (like button presses or sensor readings) in real time without constantly checking them in the main program loop. This improves performance and responsiveness.

4. **Optimize I/O Operations**:

- o **Use Efficient Communication Protocols**: For projects that involve communication between devices (e.g., I2C or SPI), minimize the number of communication operations. For example, when using an I2C LCD, ensure you don't call the `lcd.print()` function unnecessarily and batch text updates whenever possible.
- o **Debounce Inputs**: When working with buttons or switches, implement a debounce algorithm to prevent multiple readings from a single press.

5. **Efficient Power Management**:

o   For battery-powered systems, optimize the code to minimize power consumption. Use sleep modes when the device is idle, reduce the frequency of updates (e.g., reading sensors only when necessary), and turn off peripherals when they are not in use.

Conclusion

In this chapter, we explored how to build more complex projects with microcontrollers, using an example where a microcontroller controls a servo motor, reads data from a temperature sensor, and displays the information on an LCD screen. We also discussed how to optimize your code for better performance, focusing on reducing delays, using efficient memory, and managing I/O operations effectively. These techniques will help you build more sophisticated systems and maximize the efficiency of your microcontroller-based projects. As you continue to experiment with microcontrollers, these skills will be essential for creating advanced and efficient designs.

CHAPTER 25

WIRELESS COMMUNICATION IN ELECTRONICS

Introduction to Wireless Communication

Wireless communication refers to the transfer of information between two or more devices without using physical wires or cables. This type of communication relies on electromagnetic waves, such as radio waves, microwaves, or infrared light, to transmit data over short or long distances. In modern electronics, wireless communication is used in many applications, from mobile phones to IoT devices, robotics, and home automation systems.

Wireless communication provides several advantages:

- **Flexibility**: Devices can be located anywhere within the signal range, making it ideal for mobile or remote applications.
- **Reduced Cable Clutter**: Wireless systems eliminate the need for extensive wiring, which reduces the complexity of installations and maintenance.

215

- **Enhanced Mobility**: Wireless devices can be easily moved without the constraint of being physically connected to a network.
- **Cost-Effective**: Reducing the amount of cabling can lower installation and maintenance costs, especially in large or complex systems.

Wireless communication technologies have evolved significantly, offering various protocols and standards tailored to different types of applications.

Basics of Bluetooth, Wi-Fi, and RF Communication

Let's look at three common wireless communication methods used in electronics: **Bluetooth**, **Wi-Fi**, and **Radio Frequency (RF)** communication.

1. Bluetooth:

- **Overview**: Bluetooth is a short-range wireless communication standard designed for exchanging data between devices over short distances (typically up to 100 meters). It is commonly used for personal area networks (PAN), such as connecting headphones, smartphones, and other peripherals.

- **Operating Frequency**: Bluetooth operates in the 2.4 GHz ISM (Industrial, Scientific, and Medical) band, which is the same frequency range used by Wi-Fi and other devices, making it susceptible to interference.
- **Advantages**:
  - Low power consumption, ideal for battery-powered devices.
  - Easy to set up with low complexity.
  - Supported by most modern devices, including smartphones, laptops, and wearables.
- **Applications**:
  - Wireless speakers, headphones, and earbuds.
  - Smart home devices like smart lights and locks.
  - Data transfer between devices like smartphones and tablets.

2. Wi-Fi:

- **Overview**: Wi-Fi is a high-speed wireless communication standard used primarily for local area networks (LANs). It allows devices to connect to the internet or local network wirelessly. Wi-Fi operates over greater distances and at higher speeds compared to Bluetooth.

- **Operating Frequency**: Wi-Fi typically operates in the 2.4 GHz and 5 GHz frequency bands, offering different trade-offs between range and speed.
- **Advantages**:
  - High data transfer rates, suitable for internet browsing, video streaming, and file sharing.
  - Longer range compared to Bluetooth, typically up to 100 meters indoors.
  - Widely supported and commonly used in homes, offices, and public spaces for internet access.
- **Applications**:
  - Home networks for connecting devices like laptops, smartphones, and IoT devices to the internet.
  - Smart home systems and appliances that require internet access or cloud services.
  - Wireless cameras, printers, and entertainment systems.

3. RF (Radio Frequency) Communication:

- **Overview**: RF communication refers to wireless data transmission using radio waves. Unlike Bluetooth and Wi-Fi, RF communication can operate at different frequencies, ranging from low-frequency (LF) to very high-frequency (VHF) bands. RF modules can be used for both short and long-range communication.

- **Operating Frequency**: RF communication operates in a wide range of frequencies, from 30 Hz (VLF) to 300 GHz (EHF). Common RF communication systems use frequencies like 433 MHz, 868 MHz, and 915 MHz for short-range communication and higher frequencies for long-range communication.

- **Advantages**:
  - Flexible range options (short, medium, and long).
  - Lower power consumption compared to Wi-Fi, especially for long-range communication.
  - Can penetrate obstacles like walls better than infrared signals.

- **Applications**:
  - Remote control systems for toys, drones, and garage doors.
  - Wireless sensors and monitoring systems in industrial IoT.
  - Communication between microcontrollers, such as using **RF modules** (e.g., **nRF24L01** or **433 MHz RF modules**).

Real-World Example: Creating a Wireless-Controlled Device

Now let's walk through an example of creating a **wireless-controlled device** using **Bluetooth**. We'll build a simple Bluetooth-controlled robot using an **Arduino** microcontroller, a **Bluetooth module** (HC-05), and a **motor driver** to control the robot's movement.

Components Needed:

- **Arduino Uno** (or similar microcontroller)
- **HC-05 Bluetooth module**
- **Motor driver (L298N or L293D)**
- **2 DC motors with wheels**
- **Chassis**
- **Power supply (e.g., 5V or 9V battery)**
- **Jumper wires**
- **Smartphone with Bluetooth capability** (for controlling the robot)

Steps:

1. **Assemble the Hardware**:
   o Mount the **DC motors** onto the robot chassis and attach the wheels.

- o Connect the **motor driver** to the motors and the Arduino. For example, use pins 9 and 10 on the Arduino to control motor A, and pins 11 and 12 for motor B.
- o Connect the **HC-05 Bluetooth module** to the Arduino. The connections are as follows:
    - **VCC** to 5V on the Arduino
    - **GND** to ground
    - **TX** of HC-05 to **RX** (pin 0) on the Arduino
    - **RX** of HC-05 to **TX** (pin 1) on the Arduino

2. **Program the Arduino**: The Arduino will be programmed to read commands sent via Bluetooth and control the motors based on those commands.

cpp

```cpp
#include <AFMotor.h>

AF_DCMotor motor1(1);   // Motor 1 connected to M1
on the motor driver
AF_DCMotor motor2(2);   // Motor 2 connected to M2
on the motor driver

char receivedData;

void setup() {
```

```
  Serial.begin(9600);        //   Start    serial
communication at 9600 baud rate
  motor1.setSpeed(255);   // Set motor speed to
maximum
  motor2.setSpeed(255);   // Set motor speed to
maximum
}

void loop() {
  if (Serial.available() > 0) {
    receivedData = Serial.read();   // Read the
incoming data

    // Control motors based on received data
    if (receivedData == 'F') {
      motor1.forward();  // Move motors forward
      motor2.forward();
    }
    else if (receivedData == 'B') {
      motor1.reverse();  // Move motors backward
      motor2.reverse();
    }
    else if (
```

CHAPTER 26

UNDERSTANDING IOT (INTERNET OF THINGS)

What is IoT and How is It Revolutionizing Electronics?

The **Internet of Things (IoT)** refers to the concept of connecting everyday physical devices to the internet, enabling them to collect, send, and receive data. These devices, often called "smart" devices or "smart objects," can be anything from home appliances like refrigerators and thermostats to industrial equipment, health devices, and even vehicles.

IoT is revolutionizing electronics by making it possible for devices to communicate and work together seamlessly. This communication is enabled through the use of sensors, actuators, communication protocols, and microcontrollers, which allow devices to interact with their environment, respond to inputs, and perform tasks autonomously or in response to user commands. The ability to control and monitor devices remotely is transforming the way we interact with technology.

How IoT is Revolutionizing Electronics:

1. **Automation and Convenience**:
   - o IoT allows devices to operate automatically, improving efficiency and convenience. For instance, smart thermostats can adjust the temperature of a home based on user behavior, saving energy while keeping the home comfortable.

2. **Data Collection and Analytics**:
   - o IoT devices continuously collect data, which can be analyzed for insights. This is especially useful in sectors like healthcare (e.g., wearable health monitors), agriculture (e.g., soil moisture sensors), and industrial manufacturing (e.g., machinery condition monitoring).

3. **Remote Control**:
   - o Through IoT, devices can be controlled remotely via smartphones, voice assistants, or other user interfaces. This has led to the rise of **smart homes**, where users can control lights, locks, security cameras, and more from anywhere in the world.

4. **Improved Decision Making**:
   - o With the data collected by IoT devices, industries and individuals can make better, data-driven

decisions. For example, IoT-based smart grids help utilities optimize energy distribution and consumption.

5. **Cost Efficiency and Resource Management**:

   o IoT helps businesses and households manage resources more efficiently. In agriculture, IoT can optimize irrigation, and in manufacturing, it can prevent machine downtime by predicting failures before they occur.

How to Build Simple IoT Projects

Building IoT projects involves combining sensors, actuators, microcontrollers, and communication protocols to enable devices to collect data, make decisions, and communicate with each other. Here are the basic steps to build an IoT project:

1. **Choose Your Components**:

   o Select a microcontroller or development board, such as **Arduino**, **Raspberry Pi**, or **ESP32**, that has the necessary processing power and communication capabilities (Wi-Fi, Bluetooth, etc.).

- o Choose sensors that will gather data from the environment, such as **temperature sensors**, **motion sensors**, or **humidity sensors**.
- o Select actuators or output devices that will respond to commands, such as **motors**, **LEDs**, or **relays**.

2. **Connect the Components**:
   - o Wire the sensors and actuators to the microcontroller. For example, you can use **digital pins** for simple on/off signals or **analog pins** for sensors that output continuous data (e.g., temperature readings).
   - o Use communication modules such as **Wi-Fi (ESP8266 or ESP32)** or **Bluetooth (HC-05)** for wireless communication between the microcontroller and other devices (e.g., a smartphone or server).

3. **Write the Code**:
   - o Use an appropriate programming environment (e.g., **Arduino IDE**, **PlatformIO**) to write the code that will control the IoT system. The code will include:
     - ▪ Reading data from sensors.
     - ▪ Processing the data (e.g., converting analog readings to digital values).

- Sending or receiving data via the internet or Bluetooth.

- Controlling actuators based on inputs or remote commands.

4. **Set Up Communication**:

   o For internet-based IoT projects, you can use **Wi-Fi** to send data to a cloud service (e.g., **ThingSpeak**, **Blynk**, **Firebase**) or a custom server. This allows you to monitor and control devices remotely.

   o If you're building a local IoT network, you can use **Bluetooth** or **RF communication** to allow devices to communicate without the need for an internet connection.

5. **Test and Deploy**:

   o Once your hardware is set up and your code is written, test your IoT system to ensure it's working as expected. For example, check that the sensor readings are correct, the actuator responds to commands, and the system can communicate with other devices.

Example: Building a Smart Home System

Let's build a simple **smart home system** that allows you to control a light remotely using an **Arduino** and **Wi-Fi**. This system will include a light, a microcontroller, and a smartphone app for control.

Components Needed:

- **Arduino Uno** (or **ESP8266/ESP32** for Wi-Fi capabilities)
- **Relay module** (to control the light)
- **Smartphone with Blynk app** (for remote control)
- **LED** or a real **light bulb** for the simulation
- **Power supply** (5V for the Arduino and the relay)
- **Jumper wires**
- **Breadboard** (optional)

System Overview:

The system will use **Wi-Fi** to control the relay, which will turn the light on or off based on commands from a smartphone app. We'll use the **Blynk app** for a simple interface, where you can press a button on your phone to control the light.

Steps:

1. **Set Up the Relay**:

   o Connect the **relay module** to the Arduino. The relay will control the light by switching it on or off when activated.

     ▪ Connect the **IN1** pin of the relay to a digital pin on the Arduino (e.g., Pin 7).

     ▪ Connect **VCC** and **GND** to the power and ground pins of the Arduino.

     ▪ Connect the **NO** (Normally Open) pin to one terminal of the light, and the **COM** pin to the power supply terminal.

2. **Set Up the Blynk App**:

   o Install the **Blynk app** on your smartphone (available on iOS and Android).

   o Create a new project in Blynk and choose the **Arduino** board (or ESP8266/ESP32 if you're using those for Wi-Fi).

   o Add a **Button widget** in the Blynk app. This button will send commands to the Arduino to turn the light on or off.

   o Note the **Auth Token** generated by the app—this will be used to link the Blynk app to your Arduino.

3. **Write the Code**:

o Use the **Blynk library** to connect the Arduino to the Blynk app. Here's an example code for controlling the relay via the Blynk app.

cpp

```cpp
#include <SoftwareSerial.h>
#include <BlynkSimpleEsp8266.h>

// Replace with your network credentials and
Blynk auth token
char auth[] = "YourAuthToken";
char ssid[] = "YourWiFiSSID";
char pass[] = "YourWiFiPassword";

int relayPin = 7;  // Pin connected to relay

BlynkTimer timer;

void setup() {
  pinMode(relayPin, OUTPUT);
  digitalWrite(relayPin, LOW);  // Ensure the
relay is initially OFF

  Blynk.begin(auth, ssid, pass);  // Connect to
Blynk server

  // Set a function to run every 100ms
  timer.setInterval(100L, checkButton);
```

```
}

void loop() {
  Blynk.run();   // Run Blynk code
  timer.run();   // Run Blynk Timer
}

void checkButton() {
  if (Blynk.virtualRead(V1) == 1) {   // If button
is pressed in Blynk app
    digitalWrite(relayPin, HIGH);      // Turn on
light
  } else {
    digitalWrite(relayPin, LOW);       // Turn off
light
  }
}
```

4. **Upload the Code**:
   - o Upload the code to your **Arduino** or **ESP8266/ESP32** board.
   - o Make sure the **relay** is connected properly and the **Blynk app** is running on your smartphone.

5. **Test the System**:
   - o Open the **Blynk app**, press the button on your phone, and check if the light turns on or off accordingly. You should be able to control the light wirelessly from anywhere, as long as both

the Arduino and the smartphone are connected to the internet.

Conclusion

In this chapter, we explored the concept of **Internet of Things (IoT)**, which allows devices to communicate with each other and the internet, revolutionizing the way we interact with technology. We learned how to build simple IoT projects, such as a **smart home system** that controls a light remotely using Wi-Fi and the **Blynk app**. The possibilities for IoT are vast, with applications in home automation, healthcare, agriculture, industrial monitoring, and more. By integrating sensors, actuators, and communication protocols, IoT empowers us to create connected systems that improve efficiency, convenience, and productivity.

CHAPTER 27

BUILDING AND SHARING YOUR OWN PROJECTS

How to Share Your Projects with Others

Sharing your electronics projects not only helps you gain feedback and improve your designs but also allows others to learn from your work and contribute to the community. Here's how you can share your projects effectively:

1. **Documenting Your Projects**:
   - Proper documentation is key when sharing your projects. This includes providing detailed explanations of your project's design, components, circuit diagrams, and code.
   - **Project Overview**: Start by explaining what your project does, what problem it solves, and the intended outcome.
   - **Step-by-Step Guide**: Provide clear instructions, including how to assemble the circuit, wire the components, and write/upload the code.
   - **Images and Diagrams**: Use photographs or diagrams to illustrate the assembly process. This

233

helps others understand how to build your project and avoid common mistakes.

- o **Code Sharing**: Share your code with comments explaining key parts. Platforms like **GitHub** are great for sharing code, version control, and collaborating with others.

2. **Online Platforms to Share Your Projects**:
   - o **Instructables**: Instructables is a popular website where creators share step-by-step instructions on building various DIY projects, including electronics. Upload your project here for visibility and feedback.
   - o **Hackster.io**: Hackster is a community of makers where you can upload your projects, collaborate with others, and get recognized for your work.
   - o **GitHub**: GitHub is an essential platform for sharing code and collaborating on open-source projects. You can create a repository for your project, allowing others to view, contribute, and improve your code.
   - o **YouTube**: Create a video tutorial demonstrating how to build and use your project. This is particularly helpful for those who learn better through visual content.
   - o **Blogs and Personal Websites**: If you have a blog or website, you can publish detailed articles and

tutorials about your projects. It's a great way to build a personal brand and connect with your audience.

3. **Creating and Sharing Files**:

   o **Circuit Diagrams**: Use tools like **Fritzing** or **KiCad** to create professional-looking circuit diagrams. These can be shared as images or PDF files.

   o **Bill of Materials (BoM)**: Provide a list of all the components used in your project, including part numbers, quantities, and where to buy them. This will help others replicate your project easily.

   o **Project Files**: Make your project files (e.g., Arduino sketches, PCB designs, or 3D models) available for download. This will enable others to modify or build upon your project.

4. **Engaging with the Community**:

   o **Forums and Online Groups**: Join forums like **Stack Exchange**, **Reddit's r/AskElectronics**, or **ElectronicsPoint** to ask questions, share your work, and collaborate on projects. These communities provide a wealth of knowledge and support.

   o **Social Media**: Share your projects on platforms like **Twitter**, **Instagram**, or **Facebook**. Electronics communities on social media allow for networking and connecting with like-minded makers and hobbyists.

Introduction to Open-Source Electronics Communities

Open-source electronics communities play a critical role in the growth and development of the maker community. By embracing open-source principles, you can contribute to and benefit from a global pool of knowledge, resources, and projects. Here's an introduction to some of the key open-source electronics communities:

1. **Arduino Community**:
   - **Overview**: Arduino is an open-source electronics platform that has transformed the world of DIY electronics. Its hardware and software are open-source, allowing anyone to modify, share, and build upon it.
   - **Community Resources**:
     - **Arduino Forums**: The official Arduino forums are an excellent place to ask questions, share ideas, and discuss projects.
     - **Arduino Projects Hub**: The Arduino website hosts a collection of community-

contributed projects with tutorials and resources.

- **Arduino Libraries**: The Arduino IDE is filled with open-source libraries, which allow users to easily interface with different sensors, motors, and devices.

2. **Raspberry Pi Community**:

   o **Overview**: Raspberry Pi is a small, affordable computer that has been widely adopted in both education and industry. The Raspberry Pi community shares a vast amount of open-source projects, tutorials, and code.

   o **Community Resources**:

     - **Raspberry Pi Forums**: A place for users to exchange ideas and troubleshoot issues.

     - **Raspberry Pi Projects**: The Raspberry Pi website features a variety of open-source projects, from home automation to robotics.

     - **GitHub Repositories**: Many Raspberry Pi projects are hosted on GitHub, allowing users to contribute to code and documentation.

3. **Open-Source Hardware (OSHWA)**:

o **Overview**: OSHWA is an organization that supports and advocates for open-source hardware projects. Their mission is to make hardware designs freely available, enabling collaboration and improvement.

o **Community Resources**:

- **OSHWA Website**: You can find a list of open-source hardware projects and resources, as well as certification programs for open-source hardware.

- **Maker Faire**: A global event where makers showcase open-source hardware projects, offering opportunities for networking and learning.

4. **Hackaday.io**:

o **Overview**: Hackaday is a website that showcases open-source hardware and software projects. Hackaday.io is a platform for creators to upload their projects, share knowledge, and collaborate.

o **Community Resources**:

- **Hackaday Projects**: A large collection of community-submitted projects that anyone can build or improve upon.

- **Hackaday Prize**: An annual competition for the best open-source hardware projects.

5. **Adafruit Industries**:
   o **Overview**: Adafruit is a company that produces open-source hardware and educational resources. Their mission is to empower makers and engineers through open hardware.
   o **Community Resources**:
      ▪ **Adafruit Learning System**: A platform with tutorials and projects, ranging from beginner to advanced levels.
      ▪ **Adafruit Forums**: A space for users to share their projects, troubleshoot issues, and learn from one another.

6. **Instructables**:
   o **Overview**: Instructables is an online community where users can post step-by-step instructions for building all kinds of projects, including electronics. It is a valuable resource for learning how to create your own open-source electronics projects.
   o **Community Resources**:
      ▪ **Electronics Projects**: Instructables has a dedicated section for electronics, with many open-source project tutorials.
      ▪ **Competitions**: Instructables hosts various contests, offering opportunities to showcase your work and win prizes.

Next Steps: Advancing Your Skills in Electronics

Once you've mastered the basics of electronics and have shared a few projects, the next step is to advance your skills. Here are some suggestions for deepening your knowledge and expertise:

1. **Learn Advanced Circuit Design**:
   - Dive into more complex circuit design, including designing **PCBs (Printed Circuit Boards)**, creating **analog circuits**, and exploring **RF circuits**.
   - Learn to use tools like **KiCad**, **Altium Designer**, or **Eagle** for PCB design.

2. **Explore Embedded Systems Development**:
   - Explore microcontrollers like **ARM-based systems**, **ESP32**, or **Raspberry Pi** for more powerful and flexible development.
   - Learn embedded **C/C++ programming** for more control over hardware.

3. **Get Into Wireless Communication**:
   - Explore wireless communication protocols like **Zigbee**, **LoRa**, and **Bluetooth Low Energy (BLE)**.

- o Work with modules like **nRF24L01, ESP8266**, or **LoRaWAN** for long-range communication.

4. **Dive into the Internet of Things (IoT)**:

   - o Learn how to integrate your devices into the cloud using platforms like **ThingSpeak, Blynk, Firebase**, or **AWS IoT**.

   - o Explore building **smart home systems, IoT sensors**, and **data logging systems** that communicate over Wi-Fi or cellular networks.

5. **Join Maker Communities**:

   - o Attend **Hackathons, Maker Faires**, and **Meetups** to network with others in the electronics and maker community.

   - o Participate in **open-source hardware** and **software** projects on **GitHub** or **Hackaday.io**.

6. **Take Advanced Courses and Certifications**:

   - o Take online courses or certifications in areas like **embedded systems, microcontroller programming**, and **circuit design**. Websites like **Coursera, Udemy**, and **edX** offer a range of courses on these topics.

Conclusion

In this chapter, we explored how to **build and share your electronics projects** with others, including platforms and communities like **Instructables, Hackster.io**, and **GitHub**. We also discussed the importance of joining **open-source electronics communities** and how they contribute to the growth of the maker ecosystem. Finally, we provided a roadmap for advancing your skills in electronics by delving into advanced topics like **embedded systems, wireless communication**, and **IoT**. By continuing to experiment, collaborate, and learn, you can grow as a maker and creator in the exciting world of electronics.